Robert Scholes
Nancy R. Comley   Carl H. Klaus
Michael Silverman

Some Suggestions for Using

Elements of Literature

Fiction · Poetry
Drama · Essay
Film

Revised Edition

Some Suggestions for Using

ELEMENTS OF
LITERATURE

20/10/82

Some Suggestions for Using

ELEMENTS OF LITERATURE

Revised Edition

FICTION	**ROBERT SCHOLES** Brown University
POETRY	**NANCY R. COMLEY** University of Oklahoma
DRAMA	
ESSAY	**CARL H. KLAUS** The University of Iowa
FILM	**MICHAEL SILVERMAN** Brown University

Please note that this instructor's manual is for use with either ELEMENTS OF LITERATURE 5 or ELEMENTS OF LITERATURE 3.

New York   Oxford
OXFORD UNIVERSITY PRESS
1982

Printing (last digit): 9 8 7 6 5 4 3 2 1

Copyright © 1978, 1982 by Oxford University Press, Inc.

ISBN 0-19-503141-5

Printed in the United States of America

Introductory Note

This booklet is designed to provide some suggestions for teachers using *Elements of Literature* as a classroom text. It is not the place to find answers to questions about the literary works included in that text. Rather, it offers some hints about possible assignments, topics of discussion, and problems that may arise in the consideration of specific essays, stories, poems, and plays, as well as some guidance for the use of the section on film.

R. S.

C. H. K.

M. S.

N. R. C.

Contents

POETRY

DRAMA

ESSAY

FILM

Some Suggestions for Using

ELEMENTS OF
LITERATURE

Fiction

ROBERT SCHOLES

THE ELEMENTS OF FICTION

INTRODUCTION (pp. 3–21)

This section of the text is designed to provide the student with three
things:
1. critical concepts and terminology that will enable him or her to analyze
   and discuss fiction seriously;
2. historical materials that will give the student some background against
   which modern fiction may be perceived; and
3. examples of critical practice that will enable students to see how profes-
   sional critics go about the act of interpretation.

The instructor can, of course, ignore all these materials and simply
"teach the stories"—but teaching the stories should be more effective and
enjoyable if judicious use is made of the materials in this section. Here are
some suggestions for their use.

These pages can simply be assigned and read as a unit, but students may
find it difficult to assimilate so many terms and concepts at once. It might
be useful to select one of the shorter stories from the *Realism* section and
consider it in relation to the various elements. The six suggestions provided on pages 10–11 for studying "plot" may mean more to a student if
class discussion focuses on a particular story in relation to each of these
six points. And this may be done with other topics as well.

The passage from Proust on page 18 is intended to provide opportuni-
ties for a writing assignment (a paraphrase) and a discussion on the metaphoric dimension of this particular passage. This examination of metaphor
should, of course, correlate with any earlier or later consideration of metaphor in poetry.

KINDS OF STORY (pp. 22–38)

Depending on the instructor's preferences, much or little may be made of
this section. It is designed to reward the instructor and students who make
much of it.

Myth The questions on page 23 can be used for written work or class
discussion. In our view a reasonable case can be made for preferring
either the plain or the fancy version of Orpheus. Students and instructors
may differ strongly on this matter. Discussion should bring out the assumptions about literary value that underlie such preferences. Our advice

is to avoid insisting on a resolution to the discussion and to encourage students to consider specific details in the light of their opinions.

Fable and Parable We advise encouraging some creative responses here, as suggested on page 26; these can then be discussed in class.

The Tale These two tales may be used to return to the critical concepts of pages 3–21, for they have all the elements of fiction discussed in those pages. The falcon as symbol, for instance, is a rich topic for consideration. Both stories also turn on relationships between the sexes—in both there are, for instance, wives/widows who are approached by potential lovers. Yet the authors seem to have different values and present the situations in terms of these values. There is much material here for thematic discussion.

TYPES OF CHARACTER (pp. 38–55)

Legendary Hero These two heroic narratives establish a pattern or formula for a certain kind of military figure. Discussion of this material should aim at uncovering the formula. Assignments might include creative mythologizing of other figures, or perhaps parodies, in which the formula is subverted for comic effect.

Social Type The questions on page 44 provide material for either written papers or class discussion. Modern versions of these types make excellent creative papers which can lead to a discussion of critical principles.

Historical Personage This is the place to focus on style and the techniques of individualizing characters. Seneca relies on speeches of a very formal kind and the reports of important actions. Saint-Simon concentrates on visual images and homely little details. Discussion should focus closely on particulars that instructor and students find to be effective or revealing.

THREE STORIES AND COMMENTARIES (pp. 56–79)

In discussing these stories and commentaries, it will be most appropriate to raise questions about the relationship between each critical commentary and the story it considers. Students should be encouraged to say which parts of the commentary seemed most helpful to them, and also to say where they felt the commentary to be inadequate or where they disagreed with the editors' analysis.

The instructor should note that the editors have taken care to provide in the "Collection of Modern Fiction" another story by each of the three authors represented in this section. It is thus possible, and would be appropriate, to assign each of these stories and commentaries *along with* a second story by the same author, giving students the assignment of providing a commentary upon the second story. In this way they will have a critical example to follow but will have to adapt it to the specifics of a "new" work. As a step in the direction of an entirely original critical interpretation, this assignment should be helpful.

A COLLECTION OF MODERN FICTION

FABULATION

NATHANIEL HAWTHORNE, "My Kinsman, Major Molineux" (pp. 82–98)

Theme: Initiation

Related Stories:

Anderson, "I'm a Fool"
Ellison, "Battle Royal"
Lessing, "Sunrise on the Veld"

Other Related Works:

Housman, "When I was one-and-twenty"
Ibsen, *A Doll's House*
Shaw, *Major Barbara*

Questions for Reading and Discussion:

1. Locate the setting as precisely as possible in time and space.
2. Much of the effect of the story depends on irony—specifically, what Robin does not know about his Kinsman and the world that everyone else does know. Where is the reader located in this ironic structure of knowledge and ignorance? Consider specific episodes, such as the episode outside the barber's shop or that of the lady with the scarlet petticoat. To what extent are these episodes, and the whole story, comic? How do you read a statement like Robin's, "For I have the name of being a shrewd youth"?
3. Consider the reappearances of characters in the story. First, make a list of all such reappearances. Then consider their meaning and effect.

Paper Topics:

1. Consider Robin's laugh at his Kinsman—"The loudest there"—in relation to the narrator's statement in the next paragraph about "frenzied merriment, trampling on an old man's heart." Considering all that comes before and after this statement, what does this laugh signify: to Robin, to the narrator, to the story, to you?
2. Consider this story in relation to one or two other stories of "initiation." What are the common features of such stories? What elements seem unique or special to each one? Consider especially the kinds of test or trial the initiate undergoes and the result. Are there happy or unhappy initiations, or do they almost always result in mixed feelings?

H. G. WELLS, "The Country of the Blind" (pp. 98–118)

Themes: Knowledge, Thought, Power, Individual *vs.* Society

Related Stories:

Vonnegut, "Harrison Bergeron"
Le Guin, "The Ones Who Walk Away from Omelas"

Other Related Works:

Molière, *The Misanthrope*
Shaw, *Major Barbara*

Comments:

This is a "thought experiment" in something like Einstein's sense of that expression—a "What if . . . ?" given fictional breadth and depth. One can profitably study its formal qualities—the techniques used to establish the non-real as believable—but these are only means to a more philosophical end. It is fiction of ideas, a sort of science fiction, and can most usefully be related to other thought experiments.

Behind this story lies not only the proverb about the one-eyed man in the country of the blind, but also Plato's fable of "The Cave," which is reproduced below and can be duplicated for your students if you wish to use it.

Questions for Reading and Discussion:

1. What is the story saying or implying about the relationship between perception and knowledge?
2. What does the story suggest about human notions of beauty?
3. What do you think of Nuñez's desire for power?
4. Evaluate Nuñez's decision to flee the Country of the Blind. Try to make the full case for both the rightness and the wrongness of his decision before setting your own views.
5. Why does the story end exactly where and when it does?

Paper Topics:

1. Write an alternate conclusion for the story. Either begin where it presently ends and add your own material or go back to some specified point in the story and provide your own conclusion. Imitate Wells's style as closely as you can, and make your continuation seem as appropriate as possible for what has gone before.
2. Compare this story to one of the other science fiction "thought experiments" in this book. Vonnegut's and Le Guin's are perhaps the most

appropriate. All of these stories are concerned with such themes as the relationships of the individual to the group, with justice, truth, and beauty. Discuss both the ideas presented and the method of presentation in both of your chosen texts.

3. Compare this story to Plato's fable of "The Cave." Wells is obviously aware of Plato, but is he saying the same thing? How do these stories differ in end and means? What techniques and values do they share? Are they both "fables" in the same sense of the word—or both "thought experiments"?

PLATO, "The Cave" (Speakers are Socrates and Glaucon)

And now, I said, let me show in a figure how far our nature is enlightened or unenlightened:—Behold! human beings living in an underground den, which has a mouth open towards the light and reaching all along the den; here they have been from their childhood, and have their legs and necks chained so that they cannot move, and can only see before them, being prevented by the chains from turning round their heads. Above and behind them a fire is blazing at a distance, and between the fire and the prisoners there is a raised way; and you will see, if you look, a low wall built along the way, like the screen which marionette players have in front of them, over which they show the puppets.

I see.

And do you see, I said, men passing along the wall carrying all sorts of vessels, and statues and figures of animals made of wood and stone and various materials, which appear over the wall? Some of them are talking, others silent.

You have shown me a strange image, and they are strange prisoners.

Like ourselves, I replied; and they see only their own shadows, or the shadows of one another, which the fire throws on the opposite wall of the cave?

True, he said: how could they see anything but the shadows if they were never allowed to move their heads?

And of the objects which are being carried in like manner they would only see the shadows?

Yes, he said.

And if they were able to converse with one another, would they not suppose that they were naming what was actually before them?

Very true.

And suppose further that the prison had an echo which came from the other side, would they not be sure to fancy when one of the passers-by spoke that the voice which they had heard came from the shadow?

No question, he replied.

From *The Republic of Plato*. Translated by Benjamin Jowett. 1908. Oxford University Press, Oxford.

To them, I said, the truth would be literally nothing but the shadows of the images.

That is certain.

And now look again, and see what will naturally follow if the prisoners are released and disabused of their error. At first, when any of them is liberated and compelled suddenly to stand up and turn his neck round and walk and look towards the light, he will suffer sharp pains; the glare will distress him, and he will be unable to see the realities of which in his former state he had seen the shadows; and then conceive some one saying to him, that what he saw before was an illusion, but that now, when he is approaching nearer to being and his eye is turned towards more real existence, he has a clearer vision,—what will be his reply? And you may further imagine that his instructor is pointing to the objects as they pass and requiring him to name them,—will he not be perplexed? Will he not fancy that the shadows which he formerly saw are truer than the objects which are now shown to him?

Far truer.

And if he is compelled to look straight at the light, will he not have a pain in his eyes which will make him turn away to take refuge in the objects of vision which he can see, and which he will conceive to be in reality clearer than the things which are now being shown to him?

True, he said.

And suppose once more, that he is reluctantly dragged up a steep and rugged ascent, and held fast until he is forced into the presence of the sun himself, is he not likely to be pained and irritated? When he approaches the light his eyes will be dazzled, and he will not be able to see anything at all of what are now called realities.

Not all in a moment, he said.

He will require to grow accustomed to the sight of the upper world. And first he will see the shadows best, next the reflections of men and other objects in the water, and then the objects themselves; then he will gaze upon the light of the moon and the stars and the spangled heaven; and he will see the sky and the stars by night better than the sun or the light of the sun by day?

Certainly.

Last of all he will be able to see the sun, and not mere reflections of him in the water, but he will see him in his own proper place, and not in another; and he will contemplate him as he is.

Certainly.

He will then proceed to argue that this is he who gives the season and the years, and is the guardian of all that is in the visible world, and in a certain way the cause of all things which he and his fellows have been accustomed to behold?

Clearly, he said, he would first see the sun and then reason about him.

6

And when he remembered his old habitation, and the wisdom of the den and his fellow-prisoners, do you not suppose that he would felicitate himself on the change, and pity them?

Certainly, he would.

And if they were in the habit of conferring honours among themselves on those who were quickest to observe the passing shadows and to remark which of them went before, and which followed after, and which were together; and who were therefore best able to draw conclusions as to the future, do you think that he would care for such honours and glories, or envy the possessors of them? Would he not say with Homer,

"Better to be the poor servant of a poor master,"

and to endure anything, rather than think as they do and live after their manner?

Yes, he said, I think that he would rather suffer anything than entertain these false notions and live in this miserable manner.

Imagine once more, I said, such an one coming suddenly out of the sun to be replaced in his old situation; would he not be certain to have his eyes full of darkness?

To be sure, he said.

And if there were a contest, and he had to compete in measuring the shadows with the prisoners who had never moved out of the den, while his sight was still weak, and before his eyes had become steady (and the time which would be needed to acquire this new habit of sight might be very considerable) would he not be ridiculous? Men would say of him that up he went and down he came without his eyes; and that it was better not even to think of ascending; and if any one tried to loose another and lead him up to the light, let them only catch the offender, and they would put him to death.

No question, he said.

This entire allegory, I said, you may now append, dear Glaucon, to the previous argument; the prisonhouse is the world of sight, the light of fire is the sun, and you will not misapprehend me if you interpret the journey upwards to be the ascent of the soul into the intellectual world according to my poor belief, which, at your desire, I have expressed— whether rightly or wrongly God knows. But, whether true or false, my opinion is that in the world of knowledge the idea of good appears last of all, and is seen only with an effort; and, when seen, is also inferred to be the universal author of all things beautiful and right, parent of light and of the lord of light in this visible world, and the immediate source of reason and truth in the intellectual; and that this is the power upon which he who would act rationally either in public or private life must have his eye fixed.

I agree, he said, as far as I am able to understand you.

FRANZ KAFKA, "On Parables," "An Imperial Message" (pp. 119–20)

Themes: Interpretation, Knowledge, Belief

Related Stories:

Parables of Jesus
Fables of Aesop
Wells, "The Country of the Blind"
Carter, "The Snow Child"
Cortázar, "Blow-Up"

Other Related Works:

Thurber, "The Moth and the Star"
Stevens, "The Snow Man"
Stevens, "Of Mere Being"

Comments:

Both of these anti-parables set out to explore and dramatize the gap between important truths and our expression of them in language. "On Parables" is a meta-parable that faces directly the question of why certain things must be expressed indirectly. "An Imperial Message" makes concrete the difficulty in receiving any information about the essence of things.

Questions for Reading and Discussion:

1. The only difficulty in "On Parables" comes in the last sentence, but it is a great difficulty. How many interpretations of what it means to "lose" in parable can each student (or a whole class) provide? What makes one interpretation more satisfying than another? Does a good interpretation "win" in reality or in parable?
2. "An Imperial Message" presents more difficulties for the interpreter:
   a. What does the Emperor represent?
   b. Why is he dying?
   c. What is the message?
   d. Who is the messenger?
   e. What makes his job difficult?
   f. What does the word "dream" in the last sentence mean?
   You understand that you are being asked to allegorize or translate the story into another, hidden significance. You must begin with some such notion as "The Emperor is God" or "The Emperor is Reality" and then make everything consistent with your beginning.

Paper Topics:

1. Compare these parables with those of Jesus. In your discussion consider the following questions. What *is* a parable? Are the notions of parable

held by Jesus and by Kafka identical? If there are differences, what are they? Is their practice as parablists different? If you were handed an unlabeled parable and told it was by either Jesus or Kafka, what qualities would you expect to help you decide who was the author?

2. Compare these two parables in form and meaning to Plato's story of "The Cave" (instructor should provide—see notes for Wells's "The Country of the Blind"). Both Plato and Kafka are using fiction to discuss the nature of reality and human perception of it. Try to describe as carefully as possible what each of them suggests to be the truth about these large matters. Ground your interpretation in the texts at every point.

3. Later writers have taken up similar questions in ways not unlike Kafka's sort of parable. Consider Thurber's "The Moth and the Star" and Stevens's "The Snow Man" or "Of Mere Being." Clearly, the manner of Thurber is very different from that of Stevens, and both of theirs from that of Kafka—but similar concerns are active in all these texts, and they even share a similar reliance on parable to convey meaning. Do not worry too much about the differences in tone and style. Try to get beyond them to explore the common themes. For instance, does the phrase "he began to think" in "The Moth and the Star" mean the same thing as "dream it to yourself" in "An Imperial Message"?

D. H. LAWRENCE, "The Rocking-Horse Winner" (pp. 120–33)

Themes: Money, Love, Family Life

Related Stories:

Maupassant, "The Diamond Necklace"
Lawrence, "The Christening"
Le Guin, "The Ones Who Walk Away from Omelas"

Comments:

This story is a kind of fable, with the moral stated by Oscar Cresswell in the closing lines. But there is more to the story than this. Cresswell's moral itself needs further interpretation. In particular we need to ask whether the story is simply about a perversion of family structure in a single family or about something gone wrong on a much larger scale. Is the gambling merely gambling or does it represent the corrupt essence of a market economy? Are the parents uniquely depraved or simply an extreme development of what everyone in their social position really desires? It is safest, perhaps, to read this as a merely moral fable, but it is hard to avoid the conclusion that Lawrence meant more than that.

Questions for Reading and Discussion:

1. Consider the moral drawn by Oscar Cresswell. Should we understand by this that Paul is too unusual, too delicate, or that there is something wrong with "life" itself, with the social fabric in which Paul had to live?
2. Consider the supernatural elements in the story. At what point do you begin to suspect that this will not be a slice of life (like "The Christening") but a work of fabulation? Analyze the opening paragraph carefully, perhaps comparing it to the first paragraph of Joyce's "The Boarding House" or to that of "The Christening."

Paper Topics:

1. Maupassant's story "The Diamond Necklace" is as dominated by money as is this one. Compare the theme of money as it appears in the two stories. How does money relate to social position? What are the drives that lead people to make such sacrifices for it? What *do* these people desire and what are the writers telling us about these desires? Are they saying the same thing or something rather different?
2. Le Guin's "The Ones Who Walk Away from Omelas" also deals with a prosperity that rests upon the suffering of a child. Both stories are fables; both mix natural and fabulous materials. Explore the two mixtures, the two treatments, the two themes. Do the two stories urge the same values? Do they make the same point in different ways or different points altogether? Try to state the moral implications of both fables as fully and delicately as you can.

ELIZABETH BOWEN, "The Demon Lover" (pp. 134–39)

Themes: Love, Death

Related Story:

Cheever, "The Swimmer"

Other Related Works: Ballads:

"The Demon Lover"
"The Unquiet Grave"

Comments:

This is a fantasy designed to produce effects of suspense and horror, a story to be felt and experienced more than one to be understood and pondered. This is a good place to consider how plot is managed to produce emotional effects.

Questions for Reading and Discussion:

1. Consider the blend of natural and supernatural elements in this tale. Where does the supernatural first appear? How is it prepared for?
2. Look at a particular moment of terror in the text (such as Mrs. Drover's look at the taxi driver's face). Consider carefully what we are shown (or told) and what, that might be shown or told, is concealed from us. Consider also how this moment was prepared for, to make the emotional effect it makes.
3. The story has a moral, of sorts. What is it and how important is it?
4. Look at K's letter. What is strange about it, possibly horrifying?

Paper Topics:

1. Compare the combination of natural and supernatural elements in this tale with that in Cheever's "The Swimmer." How does the supernatural enter each tale? How is it prepared for? Try to take your conclusions toward some generalization about what makes for effective use of the supernatural in fiction.
2. Compare this story to the ballad of the same name and the related ballad, "The Unquiet Grave." Assuming that Bowen knew the old ballads (a very reasonable assumption), what has she taken from them, what has she avoided, and how has she transformed her borrowings? In answering this question, consider such matters as characterization and motivation in particular.

J. L. BORGES, "The Lottery in Babylon" (pp. 140–45)

Themes: Chance, Order, Fiction, Truth

Related Stories:

Wells, "The Country of the Blind"
Kafka, "On Parables," "An Imperial Message"
Borges, "The Theme of the Traitor and the Hero"
Le Guin, "The Ones Who Walk Away from Omelas"

Comments:

Like the other stories mentioned above, this is a thought experiment, a fiction that uses the formula "What if . . . ?" as a way of speculating about what is. In this instance Borges is playing with the notions of chance and necessity, life and art, order and chaos. This is, in fact, a kind of parable in which Babylon stands for the world, the Company for God, and so on. But it is not a closed parable like those of Jesus. It is more like those of Kafka, whose name is buried in that of the "sacred latrine" mentioned in the story.

Questions for Reading and Discussion:

1. Locate as precisely as you can the point in time and space at which the narration is made. Where is the narrator? Where has he been; where is he going? And when does he narrate: in ancient times or now? Present textual evidence for your views on this matter.

2. Summarize the history of the lottery from its first appearance to its latest development. Stick to the mechanics of its operation rather than interpretations of its meanings to the extent that you can. At what point do the actual details of operation seem to *require* interpretation in order to exist as details?

Paper Topics:

1. Taking this and the other Borges story in the collection together, try to establish a clear view of the way Borges writes fiction. What is special about his treatment of plot and character? What is unique about his relationship to the realistic and fantastic possibilities of fiction? What are his favorite themes? What are his values? If someone said they had experienced something like a Borges story, what would you understand as the quality they had experienced?

2. Compare this story to one or more of the other thought experiments in the collection—by Wells, Vonnegut, or Le Guin. In doing this try to establish the features that distinguish the thought experiment from other kinds of fiction in general, and the special qualities that make each writer's work unique *within* the common class or subgenre of fictional thought experiment.

3. Compare this story in technique and ideas to the parables of Kafka. How do both of these writers present their ideas and what ideas do they care about most?

BERNARD MALAMUD, "The Magic Barrel" (pp. 145–59)

Themes: Love, Desire, Marriage

Related Stories:

   Maupassant, "Moonlight"
   Joyce, "The Boarding House"

Comments:

This story is about the nature of desire. What Finkle wants finally is not just beauty or youth or intelligence; it is regret, suffering, fear, evil, difference from himself. And these are what he finds—or what Salzman, perhaps a consummate artist, persuades him to want and find. Perhaps his desire is not his own but the product of this imperfect magician who has created it with his own desperate art.

Questions for Reading and Discussion:

1. What are the motives behind Finkle's choice of Stella? This is a complicated question. It will need discussion.
2. What is Salzman's role in all this? How responsible is he for what has happened?
3. What do you know about Stella's character? What does it mean that Finkle expected her to have a red dress but she had only red shoes?

Paper Topics:

1. Compare the matchmaking in this story with that in Joyce's "The Boarding House." Do Mrs. Mooney and Salzman have anything in common? What about Polly and Stella? Do the writers seem to have similar or different notions of love and marriage—of life and art?
2. Love and desire have been themes of poetry and fiction for centuries. Writers have developed attitudes ranging from the cynical to the sentimental, and sometimes complex combinations of the two. Consider the theme of love as it is presented by Malamud in this story, Maupassant in "Moonlight," and some of the following poets: Donne (love poems), Herrick, Marvell, Browning ("The Lost Mistress"), Yeats ("For Anne Gregory," "After Long Silence"), Robinson ("Eros Turannos"), Cummings ("somewhere I have never travelled"), Auden ("Lullaby"), Roethke ("I Knew a Woman"), Levine ("For Fran").

JOHN CHEEVER, "The Swimmer" (pp. 159–69)

Themes: Suburban Life, Change, Social Position

Related Stories:

Lawrence, "The Rocking-Horse Winner"
Fitzgerald, "Babylon Revisited"
Bowen, "The Demon Lover"

Other Related Works:

Lowell, "Skunk Hour," "Water"
Levine, "Hold Me," "No One Remembers"

Comments:

Cheever is thought of as a realist but several of his finest stories, including this one and "The Enormous Radio," blend fantasy with realism to produce fabulation. All the fantasy in this story consists of one thing—allowing an acceleration in time to occur while the protagonist seems to be living at the normal pace. The double time-scheme allows Cheever to consider questions of class and value while telling an apparently seamless story of an afternoon's escapade.

Questions for Reading and Discussion:

1. At what point does the supernatural or fantastic enter the story? When do you *know*—and what, if any, were the preceding hints about this?
2. While Neddy is swimming time speeds up. Try to determine from the clues in the story all the things that happen in Neddy's life while he is swimming. List every event relating to him or his family that you can infer from the text.

Paper Topics:

1. Consider the use of the supernatural in this story, "The Rocking-Horse Winner," and "The Demon Lover." Are these writers using this device for similar ends or rather different ones? Try to organize the three stories in some way which will clarify the manner and purpose of the supernatural in each story. Does it make sense to begin with the notion that Lawrence and Cheever are doing something similar thematically but that Bowen and Cheever are closer in the way they use the device of the supernatural? If not, how do *you* see these relationships?
2. Like Cheever, Fitzgerald in "Babylon Revisited" is concerned with the passage of time. It is almost as if time is a force in these stories, causing things to happen which cannot be undone. Discuss the uses of time in the two stories, both as a device and as a theme. Try to establish the special quality of each story while seeking for common formal or thematic elements among both of them.
3. Compare the treatment of the passing of time, change, and human values in this story and two or more (at least one by each poet) of the following poems: Lowell's "Skunk Hour" and "Water," Levine's "Hold Me" and "No One Remembers." The techniques and situations are different, but many of the concerns are similar. What common ground can you find among these works? How does poetic exploration of a theme differ from fictional? How much do differences in social and ethnic background matter in the ways these writers treat similar material?

KURT VONNEGUT, JR., "Harrison Bergeron" (pp. 170–75)

Themes: Equality, Freedom, Individuality

Related Stories:

    Wells, "The Country of the Blind"
    Borges, "The Lottery in Babylon"
    Le Guin, "The Ones Who Walk Away from Omelas"

Other Related Works:

Shaw, *Major Barbara*
Brecht, *The Three-Penny Opera*
Auden, "The Unknown Citizen"

Comments:

This is a science fiction thought experiment, based on the actual carrying out of the American ideal of equality. What if we made a real attempt to make all citizens completely equal? That is the question posed and answered by this fable. Like most works of this kind, this one should be used to open discussion on its ideas and attitudes, rather than as an object to be studied for its own sake.

Questions for Reading and Discussion:

1. What is the moral of this fable?
2. Is Vonnegut attacking the concept of a democratic society in this essay? Is this an argument against socialism in favor of free enterprise? How does the language of empire (Emperor, Empress, barons, dukes, earls) fit into the argument of the story?
3. How does this text seek to control and manipulate your responses? What words and phrases call up your sympathetic or antipathetic feelings?
4. Suppose that when Harrison removed the mask from the ballerina she had proved to be plain, or disfigured. How would that affect the story?

Paper Topics:

1. Compare the attitude developed in this story toward human equality and inequality with that of another fictional thought experiment: Le Guin's "The Ones Who Walk Away from Omelas." Are the values of the two stories in harmony or in conflict with one another? Take care in drawing out the implications from the two texts that you do not distort what seem to be the intentions operating in each story.
2. This story and "The Lottery in Babylon" by Borges both use a fabulous situation to raise philosophical questions about the nature of existence and human values. Discuss the values developed in each story. Try to relate them as opposed, similar, or complementary. Remember to distinguish between the things each text implies about the way the world is and the way it ought to be.
3. Questions of individuality, sociability, superiority, inferiority, conformity, and rebellion come up in this story and in Wells's "The Country of the Blind." Consider what each story seems to be saying about these matters in relation to the others. Where does each author stand on such issues as the group versus the individual and conformity versus rebellion? Are they in complete agreement, partial agreement, or disagreement?

URSULA K. LE GUIN, "The Ones Who Walk Away from Omelas" (pp. 175–81)

Themes: Justice, Idealism

Related Stories:

Borges, "The Lottery in Babylon"
Hughes, "On the Road"
Vonnegut, "Harrison Bergeron"

Other Related Works:

Shaw, *Major Barbara*
Brecht, *The Three-Penny Opera*

Comments:

This is a fable or parable, based on an idea that has been familiar to philosophy for some centuries. It turns up in Dostoevsky's *The Brothers Karamazov* but the direct source, as Le Guin indicates, is from William James: an essay called "The Moral Philosopher and the Moral Life." Here is the crucial passage:

> Or if the hypothesis were offered us of a world in which Messrs. Fourier's and Bellamy's and Morris's utopias should all be outdone, and millions kept permanently happy on the one simple condition that a certain lost soul on the far-off edge of things should lead a life of lonely torment, what except a specifical and independent sort of emotion can it be which would make us immediately feel, even though an impulse arose within us to clutch at the happiness so offered, how hideous a thing would be its enjoyment when deliberately accepted as the fruit of such a bargain? . . . All the higher, more penetrating ideals are revolutionary. They present themselves far less in the guise of effects of past experience than in that of probable cause of future experience, factors to which the environment and the lessons it has so far taught us must learn to bend.
>
> (Quoted by Le Guin in *The Wind's Twelve Quarters*)

Questions for Reading and Discussion:

1. This story is governed by two impulses: the metafictional and the fabulative. There is a fable here, about justice and ideals: the story of a scapegoat; and there is a metafiction as well: a work which invites the reader to participate in the construction of an ideal place. First, locate some instances of each impulse at work. Then, consider why they are present *together*, what they do for one another. Look especially at the passages which raise the question of the reader's belief in the story.

2. Consider the passage from William James which gave Le Guin her theme. (Your instructor will provide this.) Le Guin calls this "variations on a theme," as a composer might, who borrows a musical theme from a predecessor and then restates it in various ways, as Brahms did, for instance, in his piano variations on a theme by Haydn. What is involved in Le Guin's reworking of this theme by James? What exactly has she done to it to make it her own? Consider your own reactions to the original "theme" and its restatement. What accounts for the difference in your experience of the two texts? Relate this to specific passages. Do they finally "say the same thing" in different ways or do they say rather different things?

Paper Topics:

1. Borges's "Lottery in Babylon" and Vonnegut's "Harrison Bergeron" are also what Le Guin calls "psychomyths"—that is, fables or parables that give to abstract themes a concreteness and complexity that they lack in themselves. Try to provide a "theme" for each of these other stories, like the theme from William James (which your instructor will provide) that is the abstraction behind Le Guin's story. Use this exercise as a point of departure for a discussion of the range and qualities of the modern fable or "psychomyth." Consider both the special features of each work and their common elements as members of the same category or class of stories.
2. Both this story and Hughes's "On the Road" are fables that have to do with justice, inequality, suffering, religion, and roads or travel. Considering some or all of these features, discuss the two works as variations on the large theme of justice and injustice in society. Look for both common concerns and individual variations in the two works.

ANGELA CARTER, "The Snow Child" (pp. 181–82)

Themes: Desire, Jealousy

Related Stories:

Lawrence, "The Rocking-Horse Winner"
Malamud, "The Magic Barrel"

Comments:

This story imitates the form of fairy tales, with magical transformations and triple repetitions. In the Grimms' tale of "The Almond Tree," a rich but childless wife is peeling an apple and "as she peeled the apple she cut her finger, and the blood dropped on to the snow. 'Ah,' said the woman, with a deep sigh, and she looked at the blood before her, and was very sad;

'had I but a child as red as blood and as white as snow!' " Carter has taken this image and turned it into a story about desire itself. The Count desires what he doesn't have. His desire causes him to imagine concretely the object that might appease it, but such an object can never satisfy. As the girl becomes clothed with the Countess's garments, the Count's emotions turn toward the Countess. The Count's sexual possession of the dead object of his own creation is an image for the unsatisfactoriness of all realizations of the imaginary. The rose is reality. It kills the imaginary, wounds the living. But the girl is already doomed when the Count's concern shifts to his wife.

Questions for Reading and Discussion:

1. Everything he encounters makes the Count think of a girl. Why? Why a girl, not a woman?
2. Explain the phrase, "She was the child of his desire."
3. What is the relationship between desire and imagination in this story?
4. What does the rose signify? Why does it prick both girl and Countess? Why does only the girl die?

Paper Topics:

1. Consider the relationship between desire and the imagination in this story and "The Rocking-Horse Winner" or "The Magic Barrel." How do the wants or needs of characters in these works relate to what they imagine as the fulfillment of their desires? Which comes first, imagination or desire? Is desire ever satisfied?
2. Compare this story with one of the Grimms' fairy tales, such as "The Almond Tree." What elements of Carter's story could appear in any fairy tale? What elements seem uniquely modern? Is the ending typical of fairy tales, or not?
3. Write an "adult tale" of your own. That is, read some of Grimms' fairy tales and then construct a modern tale out of some traditional material and some modern touches of your own.

REALISM

GUY DE MAUPASSANT, "The Diamond Necklace" (pp. 184–90)

Themes: Money, Social Position

Related Stories:

  Boccaccio, "Federigo and Giovanna"
  Maupassant, "Moonlight"
  Lawrence, "The Rocking-Horse Winner"

Other Related Works:

Shaw, *Major Barbara*
Brecht, *The Threepenny Opera*

Comments:

This story is similar in plotting to Boccaccio's "Federigo and Giovanna." The similarity lies in the way each leads to an ironic disclosure at the end, though they are quite different in tone. Thematically, this is related to Lawrence's "Rocking-Horse Winner," which is dominated by money, though in a different way, and to other stories and plays that explore matters of class differentiation. Her work gradually drives Mme. Loisel out of the middle class, changing her manners, making her a different person.

Questions for Reading and Discussion:

1. Consider the motivation behind the initial action of the plot. Why does Mme. Loisel *want* to borrow the necklace? And what is its effect upon her at the dance? From your examination of these matters what conclusions can you reach about her character, about the world she lives in, about Maupassant's view of life?
2. Consider the changes wrought upon the Loisels by ten years of labor. What effect does their work have upon them? What does this tell you of Maupassant's values? To what extent do you find them acceptable?

Paper Topics:

1. Consider one or two other stories that are structured around an ironic revelation in the last lines (such as Boccaccio's "Federigo and Giovanna" [pp. 34–38] or O. Henry's "Gift of the Magi"). In what ways do their similar structures make them similar stories? How do they differ? How do you account for the difference?
2. Compare this to Maupassant's other story in this collection ("Moonlight"). They are obviously different in subject matter, but similar in other respects. Considering these other matters (style, tone, values, etc.), try to arrive at a good description of the qualities that would be implied in statements like the following: "Something happened to me that was like a Maupassant story"; or, "He is trying to write in the manner of Maupassant." What would "Maupassant" mean in these instances?
3. Consider the themes of social class and money as they are treated by Maupassant in this work and either Shaw or Brecht in their plays. Discuss the values or attitudes generated toward these matters by both texts and the means used to generate them. How many of the differences you find are matters of the formal properties of the story and the play; how many can be traced to the different authors, writing in different times and places?

KATE CHOPIN, "The Story of an Hour" (pp. 191–93)

Theme: Marriage

Related Story:

Porter, "Rope"

Other Related Works:

Ibsen, *A Doll's House*
Rich, poems

Comments:

No need to ask why this story, written in 1894, has become, like Chopin's novel *The Awakening,* an important work for feminist critics. In reading the story it is essential to note that Louise has had a "good" marriage with a man described as kind, tender, and loving. This, in fact, is what makes the story interesting, for feminists and others alike.

Questions for Reading and Discussion:

1. What, precisely, is at stake here? What sort of marriage did Louise Mallard have and what are her full feelings about it? Base your responses on specific textual details.
2. How do you interpret the last sentence? What sex are the "doctors," do you suppose?

Paper Topics:

1. Porter's "Rope" presents us with a young couple interacting, without much commentary from any narrator or interpreter. Chopin's story gives us a wife alone, interpreting her marriage for herself—and, of course, for us as well. Do these stories connect? That is, do you find it reasonable to speculate that the young woman in "Rope" might someday look back upon her marriage as Louise does upon hers? Base your discussion on evidence provided by the two stories, extending your inferences only as far as seems reasonable.
2. Ibsen's *A Doll's House* treats the theme of marriage at much greater length. Discuss the views of marriage implied by both works. To what extent can we say that Ibsen and Chopin share the same view of marriage? Where, if at all, do they appear to differ? If you, personally, feel these views need to be corrected, explain the basis for your feelings and discuss the way they affect your reading of these works.
3. The poems of Adrienne Rich in this collection (except the last two) deal with aspects of married life. Taking them as representative of contem-

porary feminism, compare them with Chopin's story. What does Rich emphasize that Chopin does not? How close are their views of marriage? You must, of course, make inferences from what is said to what is implied, but try to ground your discussion in the texts themselves.

ANTON CHEKHOV, "Heartache" (pp. 193–98)

Themes: Loneliness, Poverty, Parental Love

Related Stories:

Joyce, "Clay"
Hughes, "On the Road"
Boyle, "Winter Night"
Olsen, "I Stand Here Ironing"

Other Related Work:

Beckett, *Krapp's Last Tape*

Comments:

The story seems to tell itself, to be a "slice of life," but it is very carefully structured, almost like a folk tale, as Iona tries to tell his sorrow three times (to the officer, the three gentlemen, the young driver) before finding a listener the fourth time.

Questions for Reading and Discussion:

1. Describe the voice in which this story is narrated. Look especially at descriptive adjectives, similes, metaphors, comments by the narrator. Do these cohere to suggest a "voice" with a personality behind it?
2. Does this story generate in you a feeling of sorrow for the "human condition" or anger at a social situation? Which do you suppose was intended?
3. Describe the process of your emotions as you read this story. Do you feel manipulated? Why or why not?

Paper Topics:

1. Compare the tone of this narration to that of Joyce in "Clay." Consider such things as degree of detachment or engagement. Examine such things as descriptions, metaphors, comments, and evaluations. Which narrator is more explicit, more intrusive? Which is more manipulative? Is one story more ironic than the other? If so, in what way—or are they ironic in different ways rather than "more" and "less"?
2. Explore the theme of parental love as it is presented in this story,

Boyle's "Winter Night" and Olsen's "I Stand Here Ironing." It is easy for such a theme to fall into triteness or sentimentality. How does each of these authors deal with this particular problem? What other qualities are mixed in with the love for the child in each story?

3. This is a story of terrible loneliness. Compare the treatment of age and loneliness in this story with that of Beckett in *Krapp's Last Tape*. If Chekhov is a "realist" and Beckett an "absurdist," what do these works enable you to say about the differences and the similarities between two works on the same theme in these different modes? Are there elements of realism in Beckett? Of absurdism in Chekhov?

STEPHEN CRANE, "The Bride Comes to Yellow Sky" (pp. 198–208)

Themes: Civilization, Changing Times

Related Stories:

Maupassant, "Moonlight"
Fitzgerald, "Babylon Revisited"
Cheever, "The Swimmer"
O'Connor, "Everything That Rises Must Converge"

Comments:

This story is so unique in its Western setting that it is difficult to relate to any one particular story in this collection. Its real affinities are to cinematic Westerns like *High Noon, The Gunfighter,* and a host of others that have borrowed its setting, characters, situations, and themes over and over again. The story itself is a remarkable achievement in its economical descriptions, its telling use of detail (as in the last sentence), and its tonal balance between comedy and sentiment. This is a good occasion for a discussion of prose style.

Questions for Reading and Discussion:

1. Consider the ending. Is it a surprise? What alternatives can you think of? How does it differ from a hundred Western films that move toward a similar confrontation? What emotions do you experience in reading the last scene? Can you say what features of the text motivate each of your responses?
2. Consider the beginning. How does Crane set a scene? Do any aspects of his description strike you as unusual? Are any details especially telling? How does he establish his characters? Are any descriptive details particularly striking?

Paper Topics:

1. Critics have frequently praised Crane for his way of writing, his style. Yet this story seems almost to tell itself, as if he simply described something that actually happened in a place that really exists. Are the critics wrong? Or is there something special about the way Crane tells his story that makes it memorable? Is this a simple story, or is it complex, subtle? Discuss certain sentences in detail to illustrate your response to these questions. Try to characterize Crane's writing style, to describe its special features.

2. One of the major themes of this story is historical and social change, specifically the civilizing of the West. Consider another story of social change (such as those by Fitzgerald, Cheever, or O'Connor listed above) in comparison to this one. Each story, of course, is localized in time and space, as it must be to make social change important, and each is in the style of a unique writer. But in each case the story develops an attitude toward the past and the new present or future that is coming into being. In comparing another story of change to this one, try to describe these attitudes as each story generates them. To what extent do they project nostalgia for what is past or passing, relief that change is coming, hope or fear for the future?

3. In this story and "Moonlight" by Maupassant, an outsider comes upon a loving couple and must readjust his attitude and behavior. Compare the situations in the two stories, with special attention to the thoughts, feelings, and attitudes of the Abbé Marignan and Scratchy Wilson.

SHERWOOD ANDERSON, "I'm a Fool" (pp. 208–17)

Themes: Initiation, Social Class

Related Stories:

Hawthorne, "My Kinsman, Major Molineux"
Welty, "Why I Live At The P.O."
Ellison, "Battle Royal"
Lessing, "Sunrise on the Veld"
Barth, "Lost in the Funhouse"

Comments:

This is to a great extent a story of voice: the voice of the narrator, who is also the main character, but who represents something more general—a peculiarly American voice. Anderson stands between Twain and a whole generation of later writers like Hemingway, Faulkner, and Sinclair Lewis who won international fame through their use of regional American voices. Here is the place to consider how this voice is conveyed, to look at the choice of words, the metaphors, and other figures of speech, the syntax, the range of dialect and register. This is also, of course, a story of initiation and can be compared to others of its type.

Questions for Reading and Discussion:

1. Consider the title. What, exactly, does it mean? Is the narrator actually more foolish or less so at the end?
2. What is the tone of the story? Is it comic or serious? If it is a mixture, can you analyze the features of the mixture? Does one element dominate?
3. If this was a fable what would be its moral? Is it a fable? Are you satisfied with the moral it seems to suggest?

Paper Topics:

1. Compare this story to "Why I Live At The P.O." with respect to its narrative voice. Both of these stories are told by American narrators who are also major characters in the events they narrate. Both are comic monologues, in which our interest is in the manner of telling as much as in the events told. Yet each is quite distinct. These distinctions are partly matters of age, sex, and region but they are also matters of character. Try to characterize each of the voices you discuss, to account for its special qualities, and to describe the effect it has on you, the reader, accounting, if possible, for the precise causes of this effect.
2. Compare this story to one or two other stories of initiation (such as those by Hawthorne, Ellison, Lessing, or Barth). Try to distinguish the special quality of each story, but within a general view of what the initiation story is like. That is, establish some general features of the initiation story—its typical plot, characters, tone—and then discuss the special quality of this story.

JAMES JOYCE, "The Boarding House" (pp. 218–23)

Themes: Seduction, Entrapment, Marriage

Related Stories:

Joyce, "Clay"
Lawrence, "The Christening"
Parker, "You Were Perfectly Fine"
Malamud, "The Magic Barrel"

Comments:

This is of course a story of entrapment: of social and religious codes conspiring with instinctual drives to reduce individual will to zero. In short, it's a work of naturalism, written in what Joyce himself called a style of "scrupulous meanness," drained of all emotion, allowing the reader's emotions to flow in along the channels laid out by Joyce's irony. Students may have some difficulties at first with point-of-view and time. It will be useful to get this sorted out before going on to thematic or stylistic matters.

Questions for Reading and Discussion:

1. There are three main sections to this story, each presented from a different character's point of view. First, locate the points in the text where these shifts occur. Then, consider the way that each character's viewpoint is presented. To what extent do we share each view or see the character from outside? How deeply into each character's consciousness does the narrative voice penetrate? What material are we given for the evaluation of each character? What are we told? How much do we infer?

2. The story leads toward a dramatic moment: Bob Doran's "speaking" to Polly. What does he say, and why does he say it? The story itself must be inferred from the somewhat reticent narration and the thoughts of the characters. Reconstruct that story as a sequence of events in chronological order. (This might make a good informal, written exercise.)

Paper Topics:

1. Compare this story to Joyce's other story in this collection: "Clay." This story is about getting married and the other about not getting married. But both are about the same aspects of Dublin life; both give us the same feeling of little people entrapped by great social and instinctual pressures. Examine the common features of the two texts, the values that are implied by them, and the techniques employed. By looking at these common features try to arrive at some general description of the Joycean short story. These are two typical selections from his only collection of stories: *Dubliners*. Considering them together, try to say what a *Dubliners* story is.

2. Dorothy Parker's "You Were Perfectly Fine" treats a similar situation in a totally different way. Compare the two stories with a view toward accounting for the great differences between them. What makes Parker's story funny and Joyce's very unfunny? Is it the treatment? If so, what features of each story typify their techniques? Or is it something in the situations themselves that makes one frivolous and one deadly serious?

D. H. LAWRENCE, "The Christening" (pp. 224–31)

Themes: Family Life, Fatherhood

Related Stories:

Maupassant, "Moonlight"
Chekhov, "Heartache"

Fitzgerald, "Babylon Revisited"
Malamud, "The Magic Barrel"

Comments:

The central topic of this story is "the special language of fatherhood" and the relationship between a father and his children. The birth of a child to an unmarried daughter brings social disgrace to the family. The daughter's father will stand godfather to the fatherless child, but the occasion causes him to make a kind of confession of the sins of fatherhood. The celibate clergyman cannot understand; the daughters are embarrassed; the father's life dominates and stunts the development of the children. This is a story almost without a plot. It is all character and theme.

Questions for Reading and Discussion:

1. Why does the brother sing the nursery rhyme about "pat-a-cake, pat-a-cake," and what does this have to do with Hilda's experience in the bakery?
2. How would you characterize the narrator of this story?
3. Explain the last paragraph. What is the function of this scene in the story?
4. How is the clergyman characterized? What is his function in the story?

Paper Topics:

1. Fatherhood is a major theme of this story. Analyze the father's prayer. What sort of language does he speak? What is the point of the prayer? Does the rest of the story support or contradict that point? Compare the treatment of fatherhood in this story to that in "Heartache," "Babylon Revisited," and/or "The Magic Barrel." Which presents the most appealing picture of fatherhood—which the truest? What elements of fatherhood are common to the different treatments? Which are unique to each story?
2. Compare the narrative voice in this story to that of Joyce in "The Boarding House." Look at the way each voice uses similes, metaphors, comparisons, adjectives, adverbs. Consider the way each voice presents information or withholds it, makes judgments overtly or covertly, comments directly or indirectly on the action. Try to characterize each narrative voice or, if this can't be done, explain why not.

KATHERINE ANNE PORTER, "Rope" (pp. 232–37)

Theme: Male/Female Relationship

Related Stories:

Chopin, "The Story of an Hour"
Parker, "You Were Perfectly Fine"
Hemingway, "Hills like White Elephants"

Other Related Works:

Lawrence, "Cocksure Women and Hensure Men"
Ephron, "The Hurled Ashtry"
Ibsen, *A Doll's House*

Comments:

This story is notable in a number of respects. Thematically, it has not lost its immediate, topical relevance. And it is worth noting in this respect that we cannot even be sure this couple is married. Stylistically, this is a *tour de force* in the use of indirect discourse for reporting both thoughts and conversation, which gives the story a distance and a presence that almost defy analysis. The effects of this are worth exploring.

Questions for Reading and Discussion:

1. Summarize what has happened here. Who was at fault, mostly, and how do you feel about the resolution of the dispute? Analyze your reaction carefully and indicate its basis in the text.
2. Is this couple married? What is the evidence for your conclusion?
3. What do you predict for the future of this couple? Why?

Paper Topics:

1. Compare this story to Hemingway's "Hills like White Elephants." In your comparison try to cover both the nature of the relationships between the two couples, and the occasion of the dispute that is at the center of each story, and consider also the rather different narrative strategies taken by the two writers: indirect versus direct discourse, for instance. Try to show what the differences are, but try also to go beyond enumeration to the reasons why each writer does what she or he does.
2. Compare this story to one or more of the others suggested in the list of related stories with respect to its treatment of the theme of male/female relationships. Do male and female writers seem to see these relationships in consistently different ways? What further conclusions can you draw from your answer to the previous question?
3. If you are using *Elements 5,* use this story, the essays of Ephron and Lawrence, and Ibsen's play as the basis for an essay on the possibilities and problems of male/female relationship. Discuss the attitudes presented by these writers and then go on to develop your own, accepting or rejecting ideas from the other writers as they accord or clash with your own.

DOROTHY PARKER, "You Were Perfectly Fine" (pp. 237–40)

Themes: Entrapment, Engagement

Related Stories:

Joyce, "The Boarding House"

Porter, "Rope"
Hemingway, "Hills like White Elephants"
Malamud, "The Magic Barrel"

Comments:

This light, amusing story should perhaps be enjoyed as comic relief, without subjecting it to heavy analytic scrutiny, but the sources of its comic effects will repay study: some have to do with style, some with the ordering of events, and some with the contrast between the two time periods (last night and this morning) and the two points of view (his and hers) in the story. Matters of design, like the near repetition of the first two paragraphs by the last two, may also be considered.

Questions for Reading and Discussion:

1. Consider the first two paragraphs and the last two. They are almost identical but not quite. They seem to say the same things but they do not mean the same things, either to the characters or to us. Explain the differences. To what extent does the humor of the story depend on these differences?
2. What sort of people are these? What kind of life do they lead? What sort of future do you expect for them? How serious *is* this story?

Paper Topics:

1. Joyce's "The Boarding House" is a story with a similar theme, a similar event (engagement) at its heart, though in both cases the event is off-stage. Yet the two stories are totally different in tone. How much of the difference is a matter of differences in the details of the two situations, in the worlds the different sets of characters inhabit, and in the style or treatment of the events? Explore each of these elements of the two stories—situation, world, and style—in arriving at your conclusion.
2. Using this story as a model, write a dialogue of your own, in which two characters discuss some recent event of importance which one remembers better than the other. Try to capture the realities of oral style with appropriate spelling and punctuation. Try to make it funny, too, if you can.

F. SCOTT FITZGERALD, "Babylon Revisited" (pp. 241–58)

Themes: Loneliness, Parenthood, Change

Related Stories:

Chekhov, "Heartache"
Lawrence, "The Christening"

Cheever, "The Swimmer"
O'Connor, "Everything That Rises Must Converge"

Comments:

This is a story of parenthood and loneliness, like Chekhov's "Heartache," but it is also a story of a particular era in American history and of a particular set of American expatriates who lived in Europe between the two world wars. It is a story of a way of life and the repudiation of that way of life, and the difficulty of changing patterns once they are established.

Questions for Reading and Discussion:

1. There is a simple story here, about a man who wants to reclaim his daughter. Trace the line of this story. How close to success does Charlie come? How close to failure? What are the decisive incidents? How are they decisive?
2. Consider the character of Charlie. What are his qualities? How do you feel about him? How does he feel about himself? How does the text seem to present him?
3. What role does the Ritz play in the story? How often does it appear? Is it just a setting or is it symbolic in some way?
4. What is the story's major theme? What are its dominant values? How are they presented?
5. Consider the father/daughter relationship in the story. How does each feel about the other? How is this established in the story?

Paper Topics:

1. Three stories in this collection that emphasize fatherhood are Chekhov's "Heartache," Lawrence's "The Christening," and this one. They are very different stories, but, taken together, they may be used as the basis for a discussion of the dimensions of fatherhood. What, in fact, can we learn from these stories about the nature of fatherhood? (Malamud's "The Magic Barrel" might also be considered here.)
2. The power of the past is a major theme in this story: the past as things done that cannot be undone, and as a set of habits or behavior patterns that seem to defy our will to alter them. Consider this theme as it appears in this story and one or both of the following: Baldwin's "Sonny's Blues," O'Connor's "Everything That Rises Must Converge."
3. The problem of irreversible historical change, on both the public scale of great events and the smaller scale of individual lives, is a theme in this story and several others in this collection. Discuss the theme as it appears in this story and Cheever's "The Swimmer." Try to keep in mind the unique features of the theme's presentation in each story while looking for any general, underlying agreements in ideas or values.

WILLIAM FAULKNER, "A Rose for Emily" (pp. 258–66)

Themes: Love, Loneliness

Related Story:

Chekhov, "Heartache"

Other Related Work:

Beckett, *Krapp's Last Tape*

Comments:

This macabre tale is a sample of what has been called Southern Gothic. It is like some of Poe's stories but instead of being set in some hothouse world of what Poe himself called the grotesque and the arabesque, this is set in a very palpable Mississippi, and put in the mouth of an obviously local narrator. By domesticating the macabre in this way, Faulkner increases its power and makes his tale re-readable, after the surprise of the last sentence has been assimilated.

Questions for Reading and Discussion:

1. Reconstruct, in chronological order, the story of Emily Grierson's life, as best you can from the things stated and implied by the narrative.
2. Consider the narrator of the story. Begin with the use of the first person plural in the first and last sentences and go on from there to construct a character based on what is said by the narrator and how it is said. What can you infer about the age, sex, history, and values of the narrator? To what extent do you feel that you share these values or reject them?
3. Is this story realistic or fantastic? How would you go about settling that question?

Paper Topics:

1. Try to rewrite a portion of this narrative from Emily Grierson's point of view, in the first person. Begin your paper with a page or two of such a narrative. Then stop, and finish your paper by a comparison of what you have done and what Faulkner did. Conclude with a discussion of what you take to be his reasons for using the voice and viewpoint that he finally chose.
2. Write an essay on the theme of loneliness as developed in this story, "Heartache," and *Krapp's Last Tape.* What methods do the different authors take to convey the pathos of lonely old age? How do they avoid sentimentality? Consider especially those aspects of each work that might be called grotesque or absurd. How do you interpret these elements?

ERNEST HEMINGWAY, "Hills like White Elephants" (pp. 266–71)

Themes: Love, Marriage, Parenthood, Change

Related Stories:

   Porter, "Rope"
   Parker, "You Were Perfectly Fine"
   Fitzgerald, "Babylon Revisited"

Other Related Work:

   Brooks, "The Mother"

Comments:

This is an unusual story in a number of respects. It is a story about abortion, written at a time when the topic was not discussed as it is now. Since some of your students may well miss the veiled allusions to this operation, you should probably point this out to them when you assign the story. Certainly, it will not mean much if they don't understand what is at stake in the dispute between the two characters. Behind the argument hover the larger themes of love, mutability, and parental responsibility. The dramatic style, with its nearly invisible narrator recording almost like a camera eye, is vintage Hemingway.

Questions for Reading and Discussion:

1. What are the man and the woman arguing about? What are the deepest, most consequential issues in their quarrel?
2. Reconstruct as much as you can of the lives of the two characters. Where have they been? Where are they going?
3. Consider the way the narrator describes the two characters: "The American and the girl with him." What can you infer from that about the narrator's position in relation to the characters?

Paper Topics:

1. There are two other stories in this collection that consist largely of dialogue between a man and a woman on an intimate subject: Porter's "Rope" and Parker's "You Were Perfectly Fine." Write a paper in which you compare the techniques of reporting dialogue in the three stories and relate them to what you take to be the major aim or purpose of each story.
2. Both this story and "Babylon Revisited" by Fitzgerald are concerned with American expatriates in Europe, but beyond that superficial similarity they are also concerned with the inexorable changes life works

upon human beings: maturity, responsibility, the fragility of love and happiness, the possibilities of loneliness and pain. Compare the two stories at their deeper thematic levels. Do you find significant differences in the way they explore these themes, or is there a common layer of values and concern buried under the strikingly different techniques of the two works?

3. Discuss the theme of abortion as it is presented in this story and Brooks's poem "The Mother." What aspects of abortion are presented in each work? What is left out? What reaction do you have to the two works? Try not to let your paper drift into a repetition of preconceived ideas.

LANGSTON HUGHES, "On the Road" (pp. 271–75)

Themes: Race, Class, Justice, Religion

Related Stories:

Ellison, "Battle Royal"
Baldwin, "Sonny's Blues"

Other Related Work:

Hughes, *Mother and Child*

Comments:

This is not merely a story of injustice or racial prejudice; it is also very much a story that confronts Christian religious institutions with Christian values and finds the institutions sadly lacking. The device of the apparently supernatural event that is finally explained within a realistic framework enables Hughes to make his critical point powerfully without giving up his naturalistic perspective.

Questions for Reading and Discussion:

1. Is the main subject of this story race or religion?
2. Consider the characterization of Jesus—his manner, his speech, the things he says. How is the biblical material adapted to fit in the story? Whose Jesus is this: Sargeant's? Hughes's? Mr. Dorset's?

Paper Topics:

1. Compare this story to the other stories about black characters by black writers. (They are listed above.) Can you detect any evolution in the treatment of race relations over those four decades of fiction? Try to consider changes in the material treated and changes in the method of treatment. (This is a major project, suitable for a long paper only.)

2. Rewrite the early part of this story from the clergyman's point of view, and the later part from the policeman's. Try to keep as much as possible in (even the vision of Jesus) while remaining faithful to the vision and voice of your narrative persona.
3. Consider Hughes's work in this study and his play, *Mother and Child*. What common qualities do you find that unite his work in these two forms? What can you say about the range of his interests and techniques? What about his emotional range?

FRANK O'CONNOR, "Guests of the Nation" (pp. 275–85)

Themes: Initiation, War, Death, Justice

Related Stories:

Hawthorne, "My Kinsman, Major Molineux"
Anderson, "I'm a Fool"
Lessing, "Sunrise on the Veld"

Comments:

This is an initiation story, like a number of others in the collection, but it is also a story that explores the theme of how institutional justice may equal personal injustice. The characters are drawn richly and strongly. The narrative voice is distinctive without being as idiosyncratic as some of the American narrators. The whole story is a bit understated until the last paragraph, when the emotion pours out in image and metaphor.

Questions for Reading and Discussion:

1. How does O'Connor establish a character? Consider each of the six characters. What sorts of attributes go with each name? How much do you know about physical qualities, background, values, feelings, and so on? Where and when do you receive this information?
2. Does the story have a plot? What sort of developmental structures do you find in it?
3. Consider the narrative voice. What are the special characteristics of this voice? Which things are national and which are personal?

Paper Topics:

1. Consider this story and Hawthorne's as stories of initiation. What do the young men in these stories learn? Do they learn from observation, mainly, or from implication in the experiences they face? Noting that the stories were written in different countries, a century apart, discuss what they nevertheless have in common. What is the role of civil strife

in each story? Why should times of civil strife lend themselves so well to stories of initiation?

2. Compare the narrators of this story and Anderson's "I'm a Fool." What do these young men have in common? What are the special qualities of each?

3. This story and Lessing's "Sunrise on the Veld" have in common a thematic interest in death as an initiation process. What other qualities do they share? What distinguishes the deaths in the two stories from one another, and the central characters' attitudes toward death?

KAY BOYLE, "Winter Night" (pp. 286–94)

Themes: Parental Feeling, Childhood, Death

Related Stories:

Chekhov, "Heartache"
Olsen, "I Stand Here Ironing"

Other Related Works:

Brooks, "The Mother"
Rich, "Night-Pieces: For a Child"

Comments:

This is one of the greatest of all Holocaust stories, partly because Boyle has found the technical means for distancing and controlling that experience. Not only does she give us not the experience itself but someone telling about it afterward; she goes on to limit this telling by the childish capacity of the audience. We fill in the gaps with our own terrible knowledge. Finally, the frame story itself, with its absent mother, the child anxious for love, is a strong story itself. The two, working together, make this extraordinary.

Questions for Reading and Discussion:

1. Try to grasp the setting and situation of this story as fully as possible. Locate the setting in time, place, and social class as accurately as you can. Describe the family background of the characters.

2. What is the relationship between the frame story (of the girl, maid, sitter, mother) and the inner story (of the other little girl)? How do the two stories make one story?

3. Assuming that the author wanted to present a story of the Holocaust as experienced by a survivor of the Nazi concentration camps, what is the effect of having the story told to a little girl? How does this affect not only our reception of the story but also the very things that can be told and those that must be left unsaid?

Paper Topics:

1. Two of the most powerful stories in this collection involve mothers and daughters. Both were written by women. Consider this story and Tillie Olsen's "I Stand Here Ironing." These stories are very different in voice, point-of-view, and in the events they recount, but at some level they share serious thematic concerns. Taking them together, as stories written by women about female characters, discuss their common qualities with a view toward locating the sources of their emotional power.

2. The theme of parental love has been a frequent subject for poets and writers of fiction. Considering this story, Chekhov's "Heartache," and the following poems—Brooks, "The Mother"; Rich, "Night Pieces: For a Child"; and Levine, "Losing You"—discuss the range of incident and emotion that writers have used in treating this theme. What seem to be common features, appearing in all of these works, and what things, if any, seem uniquely the province of particular writers?

EUDORA WELTY, "Why I Live at the P.O." (pp. 295–305)

Themes: Family Life, Jealousy

Related Stories:

   Anderson, "I'm a Fool"
   Lawrence, "The Christening"

Comments:

This is perhaps the funniest story in the book. The humor lies partly in the situations and characters, but mainly in the narrative voice of the postmistress. The story itself is a variant of the Prodigal Son parable, and should be compared to the original. This version, of course, is told by the child who has not become a prodigal, and all the envy and sense of injustice one might expect is in her voice—along with other things, of course, including jealousy, wit, and high spirits.

Questions for Reading and Discussion:

1. Reconstruct the crucial events in the lives of Stella-Rondo and her sister as far as you can do so from the evidence in the story. Make sure Mr. Whitaker's role is clear.
2. Characterize the narrator as thoroughly as possible. Make a list of her qualities—physical and mental—insofar as they are evident in the story.

Paper Topics:

1. Compare the use of narrative voice in this story to that in Anderson's. These are both strong American ways of speaking and thinking, but

they are very different. Can you find any common qualities? What makes them interesting?

2. Despite the differences in style and technique, this story and Lawrence's "The Christening" treat very similar thematic material. Beneath their surfaces, can you find the themes that link the stories and discuss this common thematic material? Aside from differences in treatment, what, if any, are the crucial differences in the values expressed or implied by the two works?

3. Re-tell this story from Stella-Rondo's point of view.

TILLIE OLSEN, "I Stand Here Ironing" (pp. 305–12)

Themes: Parental Responsibility, Love

Related Stories:

Lawrence, "The Christening"
Boyle, "Winter Night"

Other Related Works:

Brooks, "The Mother"
Rich, "Nightpieces: For a Child"

Comments:

There are some stories that just blow commentary—and commentators—away. This is one of them. It seems to pour out artlessly, taking its power from its material directly, like a drink from a pure spring. But it is a work of consummate art. Sincerity without art produces unconvincing texts, alas. Sincerity with commensurate art can be an awesome force. This is a voice story, in part, but the voice is perfectly balanced between the details of a particular history and the universal features of motherhood.

Questions for Reading and Discussion:

1. This story seems artless, but consider the similes in the first and last paragraphs as a way into the art of this writing. How do they function to enrich meaning, to unify the story, and to contribute to the sense of artlessness the story conveys?

2. The story is a sort of monologue. What exactly is the situation of the speaker? Who is the listener? Where? How does this device of making the listener a specific person function in the story? How does it affect *our* role as listeners or readers?

3. Try to sort out the major events of Emily's life (and her mother's) and make a chronological table of them. How would *you* sum up this life?

4. The story is also a piece of persuasive writing. The speaker is construct-ing an essay, an argument. What is the conclusion? Do you agree with it?

Paper Topics:

1. Compare this monologue with the words of the father in Lawrence's "The Christening." These two texts can be read, in part, as confessions or apologies for motherhood and fatherhood. Explore the two stories from this perspective, developing your own thesis about the two apolo-gies and what they tell us about the nature of the two conditions they represent.
2. Taking motherhood as your theme, explore the concept as it is pre-sented in this work and in those by Boyle, Brooks and Rich mentioned above. You need not give a full interpretation of each story; simply select from each the material most relevant to the theme of mother-hood, and build your discussion on this material. Your selection, of course, must be made with an awareness of the meaning of this the-matic material in its context.

RALPH ELLISON, "Battle Royal" (pp. 312–25)

Themes: Race, Initiation

Related Stories:

> Hawthorne, "My Kinsman, Major Molineux"
> Hughes, "On the Road"
> Baldwin, "Sonny's Blues"
> O'Connor, "Everything That Rises Must Converge"

Other Related Works:

> Brooks, "The Lovers of the Poor"
> Hughes, *Mother and Child*

Comments:

Ellison heightens with just a touch of the fantastic the material he uses in this story, carefully keeping it somewhere just on the fabulative side of realism. He describes events that are typical of their time and place, but with a coloring at once comic and nightmarish that marks the material as his own.

Questions for Reading and Discussion:

1. Consider the two episodes involving the narrator's grandfather. Why are they placed as they are and what is their significance?

2. What is the function of the episode involving the blonde? What is its meaning?

Paper Topics:

1. Consider this story and "My Kinsman, Major Molineux" as classic American stories of initiation. If initiation is a fall from innocence into knowledge, what constitutes innocence and knowledge for each writer? Compare the two works with respect to the use of fabulous or fantastic material, the notions of "reality" that prevail, the treatment of sex, politics, and other thematic matters that seem important to you.
2. Using this story, Langston Hughes's story and play, Baldwin's story, and Brooks's poem, "The Lovers of the Poor," as your source material, write an essay on race relations in the U.S.A. There is a place in such an essay for your own views, but try to relate them to the views presented in the texts. To do this, you will have to interpret the texts first. (This is a substantial project for a long paper.)

DORIS LESSING, "Sunrise on the Veld" (pp. 325–32)

Themes: Initiation, Death, Fate

Related Stories:

Hawthorne, "My Kinsman, Major Molineux"
O'Connor, "Guests of the Nation"

Comments:

This is a straightforward little story of initiation or maturation. Its great strength is in the descriptions of natural, physical things, and in the way the experience is gradually brought home to the boy and left unresolved, working in his mind.

Questions for Reading and Discussion:

1. Why doesn't he kill the buck? How do you feel about his decision?
2. The story is left open, in a sense: "he was by no means finished with it . . ." What do you expect him to decide when he thinks about it "the very next morning"? Or will he have forgotten?

Paper Topics:

1. Frank O'Connor's "Guests of the Nation" is another story of a young man's encounter with death. The stories are different in many ways, of course, but both involve the confrontation with suffering and death, as well as the contrast between immediate personal responses and larger

political or ecological views. Discuss the two stories as stories of maturation. What are the issues that are faced or not faced by the young men involved? What does each story say about death and maturity?

2. Hawthorne's "My Kinsman, Major Molineux" and Ellison's "Battle Royal" are also stories about the initiation of young people, but these are cultural initiations rather than natural ones, as in this story. Are there resemblances, nonetheless? Discuss the three works as initiation stories, noting the important differences but concentrating on the common features and concerns that link the three as stories that mark a significant stage in the passage from youth to adulthood.

JAMES BALDWIN, "Sonny's Blues" (pp. 332–59)

Themes: Family, Music, Race, Drugs

Related Stories:

Fitzgerald, "Babylon Revisited"
Hughes, "On the Road"
Olsen, "I Stand Here Ironing"
Ellison, "Battle Royal"

Other Related Works:

Brooks, poems
Hughes, *Mother and Child*

Comments:

This is a full rich story, almost a novella, that takes time to develop. It works with two great themes, family feeling—in this case brotherly love— and the expressive potential of art—in this case music, blues. Sonny's blues are the blues he has—his life—and the blues he makes—his music. In this work Baldwin has erected his own monument to all those black singers and musicians who made the blues out of the blues, whose heritage of misery and oppression gave them the material and the impetus to create a music that could express their experience and heritage in such a way as to do it justice.

Questions for Reading and Discussion:

1. What is meant by the word "blues" in the title? What are Sonny's blues?
2. How would you characterize the relationship between Sonny and his brother? How does it change during the story?
3. How many song titles, phrases from songs, references to musicians can you find in this story? Make a list. Try to identify everything and see

how it fits in. And while you're at it, look up the words to *Am I Blue?* How do they fit in?

Paper Topics:

1. At first glance this story and Olsen's "I Stand Here Ironing" might not seem to have much in common. But both are about the concern of an older family member for a talented but vulnerable young one. Explore the two stories together. What other thematic connections can you find? The stories have a comparable emotional power, too. How do you account for that?

2. The climax of this story is, of course, the moment in the last scene when Sonny plays the piano. Look at this episode again—the last few pages of the text. Study the verbal resources Baldwin brings to bear on the description of the music and the playing. Begin with "All I know about music . . ." and work through to the end. Look at the descriptions, analogies, comparisons, metaphors, allusions, and the final image of the glass of Scotch and milk on the piano. What can you say about Baldwin's aims in this passage? What is he attempting? What are his methods? What has he achieved?

3. Compare this story to Fitzgerald's "Babylon Revisited." Both stories treat the theme of return to a place of defeat, of facing the past in the present. Given this similarity, explore the differences in the two treatments of this motif.

4. See "Battle Royal," question 2.

FLANNERY O'CONNOR, "Everything That Rises Must Converge" (pp. 359–73)

Themes: Race, Identity, Initiation, Change

Related Stories:

Hawthorne, "My Kinsman, Major Molineux"
Ellison, "Battle Royal"

Comments:

This story is a careful and intricate blend of social questions—race, class, mobility—and family or personal questions—mother/son interaction, personal identity. The eye of the narrator is remorseless. The tone of the narration is a blend of light comedy, pathos, and satiric malice.

Questions for Reading and Discussion:

1. What is the significance of the title?
2. How would you describe the relationship between Julian and his mother?

3. Julian has more "enlightened" views than his mother on racial matters. He is better educated. Is he a better person?
4. Julian lectures his mother after she gets up from the sidewalk. Is he right in what he says? Is he right to say it? What clues does the text give us on these matters, if any?

Paper Topics:

1. Consider this story with Hawthorne's "My Kinsman, Major Molineux" as two stories of initiation. The young men in both stories pass from a state of innocence to experience as a result of observing something terrible happening to an older relative. But in other respects the stories seem quite different. Try to discuss exactly what it is that each young man learns—or that we learn from observing his experience.
2. Compare this story to Ellison's "Battle Royal." Both are stories of initiation, and both involve questions of race and identity, but the authors are situated on different sides of the racial divide, and the stories consider the questions from those different sides. What does each tell us about race, and what understanding can we gain from considering them together?

METAFICTION

JULIO CORTÁZAR, "Blow-Up" (pp. 375–86)

Themes: Fiction, Truth, Appearance and Reality

Related Stories:

Borges, "The Theme of the Traitor and the Hero"
Barth, "Lost in the Funhouse"
Coover, "The Hat Act"

Comments:

This story poses and enacts the problem of how to write. It is a problem complicated by time. One writes at one time of events that are supposed to have happened at another. Thus one is always including things from the writing time in among the things of event time. The clouds of now may help to give solidity to the scene of then. One also includes one's feelings and thoughts of the present. There is also the question of the reality of events told in a story. Even if the text begins as a report on actual events it can never stay that way. The eye (I) that saw them is dead; another I (eye) sits at the typewriter and looks out the window.

There are also the esthetic choices: does one refer to the central character or another as I or he? For an event imperfectly seen and less perfectly understood—even if it was quite real and complete in itself—forgotten details must be remembered or supplied; missing pieces—interpretations, thoughts, motives—must be supplied. No honest writer could write at all without the kind of hesitations and false starts enacted in this story.

Questions for Reading and Discussion:

1. We have two main sets of events here at two times. First, a man saw something happen that involved a boy, a woman, and a clownlike man and photographed part of that event. Second, this man, Roberto Michel, sits at his typewriter and tries to put what is left of the event (in his mind, on his film) into a sequence of words. "Michel is guilty of making literature."

   a. Sort out what we "know of both orders of events," with the different possibilities if there are more than one and the relative probability of each.

   b. Discuss the phrase, "Michel is guilty of making literature." What is its full meaning in context? What is Cortázar guilty of?

   c. Try to formulate the moral or thesis of the story, if it has one.

Paper Topics:

1. Consider this story and "Lost in the Funhouse" together. Both stories are experiments in metafiction, but they are rather different in technique. They both raise questions about the nature of fiction and draw attention to the strategies of fictional composition—but they emphasize different things. In comparing the two stories try to clarify which aspects of fiction each story is most interested in exploring as a problem for writer and reader: plot, character, style, point-of-view, time—or what?

2. Select a single paragraph of reasonable size and write a commentary on each sentence in that paragraph, explaining how it contributes to the various concerns of the story—plot, characterization, thematic development, and so on. You may include a metacommentary on your commentary, if you wish.

JOHN BARTH, "Lost in the Funhouse" (pp. 386–406)

Themes: Fiction, Love

Related Stories:

Anderson, "I'm a Fool"
O'Connor, "Guests of the Nation"
Cortázar, "Blow-Up"

Comments:

This is both a portrait of the artist as a young man and a metafiction. The metafictional elements are the things that may at first confuse or dismay student readers. I suggest that you tell them to think of the narrator as someone who has been subjected to too many creative writing courses. He can't get their advice out of his head, with the result that he often incorporates pieces of that advice in his text, or adds irrelevant examples of such advice. He gets self-conscious and puts in "literary" expressions which clash with his more natural prose. He also rebels against all advice and does as he pleases much of the time. The result is a story which parodies how-to-write-fiction courses and gains in realism by doing so. That is, the events do appear more real because they seem to have an existence independent of the text, which is clumsily trying to set the events down in words. At the same time, the story confronts the real problems of fictional narration, of capturing "reality," of gratifying audiences, of turning life into a funhouse. The story also suggests that failure in life—and especially in love—may be a prerequisite for being a writer.

Questions for Reading and Discussion:

1. Take a paragraph like the fourth one: "Description of physical appearance. . . ." Look at each sentence to determine its function. Some are metafictional, and seem to come from some textbook on writing. Some are simply attempts at fictional description which are rejected and left unfinished. Are there other kinds? What is the effect of this interaction?
2. Sort out the major events in the life of Ambrose in chronological order. You need not go back to the time of Charles I for his English, Welsh, Bavarian, and Swiss ancestors, as he does in the paragraph that begins, "Under the boardwalk. . . ." Just work through his life and this day. Make a kind of chart of the key events. He also projects his possible future. Perhaps you should note this, too.
3. Consider the first and last paragraphs. What has happened on this day? What does the funhouse symbolize, anyway?

Paper Topics:

1. Taking this as a story of initiation, compare Barth's treatment of that theme to Anderson's in "I'm a Fool." Try not to be distracted by the obvious stylistic differences, but concentrate on what events contribute to the learning experience and how the two writers develop such contrasts as truth vs. fiction and art vs. life. Suppose Ambrose and Anderson's young man both grew up to be writers; what kind of works do you think they would each write?
2. (See question 2 for "Blow-Up.")

ROBERT COOVER, "The Hat Act" (pp. 406–19)

Themes: Art, Performance

Related Story:

Vonnegut, "Harrison Bergeron"

Comments:

This is a very special kind of fiction. The events narrated are not simply fantastic but are impossible. They are not merely impossible, but impossibly impossible, as one impossibility is piled on top of another. The format, of course, of the stage magician and his audience, is a familiar one, that pre-pares us for the illusion of impossibility. But Coover forces us to face the difference between verbal illusion and dramatic illusion. He can make *any-thing* happen on his stage. He is testing the limits of verbal illusion, making the reader face the unreliability of language as a vehicle for experience.

Questions for Reading and Discussion:

1. At what point is it clear that this is no ordinary magic show? Why?
2. Read the story just noticing what the audience does, *as* an audience, ignoring what happens on the stage. Does the audience do anything impossible? Improbable? What is the function of the audience in the story?
3. Compare this to what you have seen of actual magic shows (or read about them). What elements of a standard performance does Coover use? What things, if any, are entirely new? What, for instance, is the relationship between the famous trick of sawing a woman in half and the things that happen in this story?
4. If you were going to make a film of this, how would you do it?

Paper Topics:

1. This story and "Harrison Bergeron" both involve a stage presentation with some fantastic events. Compare the use of the fabulous in the two stories. First consider what the fantastic events in each story actually are; then consider the question of the function of fantasy in the two stories. This should lead to a contrast between the ultimate purposes of the two works. Do the terms fabulation and metafiction help clarify the difference between the stories? Do the stories help clarify the terms?
2. Write a story of your own in which the impossibility of the events is a major part of the story. See what you can find to fulfill the function of the audience in Coover's story.

Poetry

NANCY R. COMLEY

THE ELEMENTS OF POETRY

FORM AND CONTENT (pp. 423–35)

If poetry is to be taught at all, something like this "Elements" section is necessary to introduce students to the analysis and interpretation of poetic materials. The section covers all the traditionally studied dimensions of poetry in language as simple and straightforward as we could make it. We recommend that it be assigned in small segments for study and discussion, more or less as outlined below.

The opening pages are general and should accomplish their introductory purpose without much discussion. With the section "Drama and Narration" we move into materials that require more detailed scrutiny. In particular, the questions on page 429 should be worked over and the comparison of the two versions of Lawrence's "Piano" developed in class, as suggested on page 432. Discussion of the movement from description to meditation in Wordsworth's sonnet on page 435 is also likely to be fruitful.

All this material may well take more than one class meeting for proper consideration.

DICTION (pp. 436–49)

The wealth of poetic examples in these pages should provide material for discussions or papers that heighten awareness of metaphor and irony as principles of language. In particular, the illustrative poems by Shakespeare (pp. 438–39), Donne (p. 440), Yeats (p. 441), Sidney (p. 444), and Knott (pp. 448–49) should be considered.

RHYTHM AND METER (pp. 449–463)

The instructor may simply follow along the text here, checking for comprehension and elaborating where necessary. As an alternative one might assign the scansion of the passages on page 460, and then in class invite students to scan different couplets on the blackboard, discussing each effort. Finally, the instructor might select a poem or two from the Selection of Poets and ask students to write a paper in which they follow the suggestions given on pages 462–63.

R.S.

Since sound is one of the major dimensions of poetry, you should always read a poem aloud to your students before discussing it. They should have practice in reading aloud as well, and if you find they've never memorized poetry before, consider including this practice.

Most, if not all, of the poetry here has been recorded. Students enjoy hearing poets read from their own work, and some poets, such as W. B. Yeats, Dylan Thomas, and Philip Levine, are powerful readers. But even less dramatic readers, such as T. S. Eliot and Wallace Stevens, are well worth listening to.

The study of poetry is greatly enhanced by having students write in some of the forms they are studying. You will find suggestions for such writing assignments at various places in this manual. Many of the assignments have proved as useful in courses emphasizing composition as they are in literature courses.

The poetry in *Elements* is arranged historically, but you may find a thematic, generic, or comparative approach more congenial. Some suggestions for such approaches are presented here.

A SELECTION OF POETS

BALLADS

Beginning the study of poetry with ballads is useful because the straightforward narratives, simple rhyme schemes, and repetition serve as a relatively easy introduction to more complex lyric poetry.

For writing assignments, students can transform ballad narratives into prose narratives, the challenge here being to fill in the gaps in the story. A reverse operation is to transform newspaper articles—especially those dealing with disasters or miserable love affairs—into ballads. Writing parodies of older ballads is also useful; for example, updating "Edward" or changing the dying cowboy in "The Streets of Laredo" to a football player or an urban cowboy. All of these ballads have been recorded, and I would suggest that students hear the sung versions to get the full flavor of the various rhythms.

"Edward" (pp. 468–69)
Version B of ballad 13 in Francis J. Child's *The English and Scottish Popular Ballads* is presented here. The question and answer technique of presentation of plot and revelation of character is more sophisticated than in most ballads. The effect of the surprise ending will probably start classroom discussion. You may want to compare the use of dialogue here with Dorothy Parker's "You Were Perfectly Fine" or Ernest Hemingway's "Hills like White Elephants" in the Fiction section of *Elements*.

"The Unquiet Grave" (p. 470)

Francis Child has a good deal to say about the background of this ballad (#78). "It exhibits the universal popular belief that excessive grieving for the dead interferes with their repose. . . ."Sir Walter Scott has remarked that "the belief that excessive grieving over lost friends destroyed their peace was general throughout Scotland. . . ." The Irish believed that "inordinate tears wet the shroud or grave-clothes," thereby making the dead unable to sleep comfortably. The "twelvemonth and a day" in the poem was considered the acceptable length of mourning.

"The Demon Lover" (pp. 471–73)

Supernatural events were popular subject matter for ballads, and the outpouring of *Rosemary's Baby*-type movies from Hollywood shows that the supernatural continues to fascinate us. This particular ballad was selected as a companion piece to Elizabeth Bowen's "The Demon Lover" in the Fiction section of *Elements*. The version presented here is slightly condensed, and if you want more details refer to the longer (32 stanzas) version A in Francis J. Child's collection of ballads.

"The Streets of Laredo" (p. 473)

The cowboy has been the American version of the mythic hero for over a century. Students might be interested in investigating other cowboy ballads—especially early ones—to get a fuller sense of the development of this myth. And since cowboys are a diminishing species (except for the urban variety), you might ask what kind of American heroes will become subjects for future ballads.

John Henry (pp. 474–75)

The version here emphasizes the struggle of man versus machine, but other versions—and there are many of them—put more emphasis on John Henry's sexual prowess, or lack of it. This is the most famous of American ballads composed by blacks for a black audience.

John Lennon and Paul McCartney, "Eleanor Rigby" (pp. 475–76)

This ballad can function as a transition to other forms of lyric poetry. How does the presentation of the story here compare with narrative presentation in earlier ballads? You might want to refer to the "Beyond Metaphor and Irony" section of the text (p. 448) before you consider this ballad, and especially if you compare it with any of the literary ballads.

WILLIAM SHAKESPEARE

A NOTE ON THE SONNET (pp. 477–80)

To quote Robert Scholes: "this is the place to really work on the sonnet. We have included sonnets among the works of many of the poets appearing in this anthology, so that time devoted to the sonnet here will pay off later on. Our emphasis on the sonnet stems from our conviction that in English poetry, mastery of this form aids in interpretation of all verse discourse." Students should try to write their own sonnets so as to get a sense of the possibilities (and problems) of this poetic form. A paragraph or two of prose can provide subject matter for a sonnet, or students can write modern versions of one of Shakespeare's sonnets. Of the sonnets here, I have found that "When, in disgrace with Fortune and men's eyes" and "My mistress' eyes are nothing like the sun" produce the liveliest results.

Note: Shakespeare's sonnet 73, "That time of year thou may'st in me behold" appears in the "Elements of Poetry" section (pp. 438–39) with a discussion of metaphor.

18 "Shall I compare thee to a summer's day?" (p. 480)

This poem is a consideration of its opening rhetorical question, comparing the variableness and ephemerality of an actual summer's day with the ideal "eternal summer" of the beloved. This eternal quality will live and be constantly renewed by those reading the lines of poetry. This sonnet can be compared with sonnets 55 and 65 as examples of one of the main themes of the entire sequence: the classical belief in the permanence of poetry, and of achieving immortality through poetry. In life beauty fades, but through poetry beauty is immortalized; poetry allows us to defy time.

29 "When, in disgrace . . ." (pp. 480–81)

The octave-sestet relationship here bears the closest reading, and students can discuss the speaker's turn from the self-obsession of lines 1–8 to love for another in the last 6 lines in terms of the poem's many verbal and conceptual contrasts: disgrace/grace; curse/blessing; outcast/kingly state; bootless cries/hymns, etc.

55 "Not marble nor the gilded monuments" (p. 481)

Here poetry as "living record" is compared with the emphemerality of princely "gilded monuments." Line 4 should be carefully considered, for as Hallett Smith has pointed out in *Elizabethan Poetry*, "sluttish time" and "unswept time" suggest "a negligent housemaid, too lazy to sweep," and thus "the aristocratic connotations of the first line of the sonnet are destroyed by the association of 'unswept' and 'sluttish.' " Note also the complex metaphors of monuments and war rising out of the statement "you shall shine more bright" in line 3.

65 "Since brass, nor stone, nor earth . . ." (p. 481)

Here too, contrasting imagery is developed in a series of four questions which are answered (provisionally) in the concluding couplet. You may want to focus on the tone of the last two lines. How confident is the speaker? How does his attitude compare with the one expressed in sonnet

18? In what ways are the connotations of "miracle" and "black" important to the tone?

94 "They that have pow'r to hurt . . ." (p. 482)

The first eight lines build toward a definition of what it means to be a lord of one's natural gifts, and introduce a comparison with those who are only "stewards of their excellence." The sestet repeats the comparison but uses the metaphor of the summer flower versus the weed. The moral issue should be considered here in light of the concluding line. You might ask students why a lily was used for comparison. What connotations do lilies have that, say, primroses do not?

130 "My mistress' eyes are nothing . . ." (p. 482)

The ironic quality of this poem is discussed on pp. 444–45 in the "Elements of Poetry" section. The poem is a parodic reply to Petrarchan sonnets, and proceeds through negations of the usual Petrarchan similes (discussed in "A Note on the Sonnet"). You might ask students to rewrite this sonnet à la Petrarch, or you might suggest they write sonnets parodying some current clichés of feminine or masculine beauty.

JOHN DONNE

From "Devotion 19" (pp. 483–84)

This passage provides an entry into the seventeenth-century mind and its religious attitudes, when it was firmly believed that the "old law was a continual allegory; types and figures overspread all." Thus, the Old Testament was read as a prefiguration of the New Testament. This might be the place to consider how metaphorical all language is—that metaphors are not limited to poetic texts. A consideration of Donne's own figures, particularly his tropes of repetition and catalogue, can provide a way into the passage. Can we find a kind of imitation of the Word at work in Donne's own style? Is God witty?

LOVE POEMS

Donne's "The Flea" is used to illustrate discussion of the conceit in the "Elements of Poetry" section, p. 440–41.

"The Good Morrow" (p. 485)

If you find that your students are shy about discussing love poems, concentrate on the stance and voice of the speaker and the ingenious developments of his arguments. The love poems presented here can be considered as different ways of defining a perfect love between man and woman. You can present them as answers to the problem of making an abstraction (perfect love) concrete.

Ask students if they would expect to find such words as "weaned," "sucked" and "snorted" in a love poem. What does such language tell us about the speaker? You should follow the development of love controlling sight (line 10) into the simile of discovery and the paradox of separate worlds yet one world of the lovers.

Notes: Line 4: The seven sleepers' den was a cave in which, according to legend, seven Christian youths hiding from the persecutions of Decius slept for over two centuries. Line 19: "Whatever dies was not mixed equally." An alchemical belief that mortality results from an imperfect or unequal mixture of elements. A perfect mixture would produce an undying substance.

"The Sun Rising" (pp. 485–86)

First, be sure students know where the speaker is located in relation to the sun. How is the sun characterized by the speaker? How does the poem reach closure? Or in other words, how does the speaker argue the sun from outside the window and into the lovers' bed, as it were? You might ask how this poem and other Donne poems conform to his statement on poetry:

> And therefore it is easie to observe that in all metricall compositions, . . . the force of the whole piece, is for the most part left to the shutting up; the whole frame of the Poem is a beating out of a piece of gold, but the last clause is as the impression of the stamp, and that is what makes it currant.

"The Canonization" (pp. 486–87)

How would you describe the speaker, and to whom is he is speaking? might well be your first questions. And you should be sure that students know the meanings of "canonization" and "canonize," for human love here meets the same demands that those declared saints meet in their response to divine love. You might also consider the poem as structured on a paradox: in stanzas 1 and 2 the lovers renounce the world, and then in the last stanza are hymned as having taken the "whole world's soul" into themselves.

"The Relic" (pp. 487–88)

Be sure that students know what a relic is, and how such things were (and are) venerated because of belief in their miraculous powers. As in "The Canonization," sacred imagery works in the service of earthly love, and this love, by which miracles were achieved, is seen as conferring immortality on the lovers. Discussion might center on the nature of the "miracles" described in the last stanza.

HOLY SONNETS

5 "I am a little world made cunningly" (pp. 488–89)

The opening metaphor, "I am a little world," refers to the Renaissance concept of the body as microcosm. The "new spheres" and "new lands" suggest the impact of Galilean astronomy in the awareness of possible worlds beyond earth. Also, the imagery of water and fire, drowning and burning, reveals the speaker's desire for a personal apocalypse.

Notes: Line 9 refers to Genesis 9:11 and God's promise after Noah that the world would not be flooded again. Lines 13–14 refer to Psalm 64:9: "For the zeal of thine house hath eaten me up." Zeal here is a healing fire, as opposed to the fire "Of lust and envy."

10 "Death, be not proud . . ." (p. 489)
You might begin by asking about the tone of the poem: how do the use of personification, the second person, frequent apostrophe, and other devices contribute to the strength and confidence of the speaker's voice? How do the tone and the use of rhetorical figures upon which it depends compare to those of "I am a little world made cunningly"? A discussion of the poem's tone can lead into a consideration of its figurative language. How, for example, can rest and sleep be "pictures"?

ROBERT HERRICK

A NOTE ON CAVALIER POETRY (pp. 489–91)

Herrick's sonnet, "I sing of Brooks, of Blossoms, Birds and Bowers," is worth attention as a good introduction to his poetry. Students should be asked to define "cleanly-wantonness," a concept which informs the tone and content of Herrick's poetry.

"Delight in Disorder" (p. 491)
You might ask students to discuss the poem's last two lines in relation to the art of poetry as well as to the art of dress.

"Upon Julia's Clothes" (p. 492)
Is it merely Julia's silks to which the speaker is responding? You might ask students to update this poem or "Delight in Disorder" with reference to today's fashions.

"To the Virgins to Make Much of Time" (p. 492)
This poem is one of the best-known examples of *carpe diem* in English. Attention to the rhythm and rhyme scheme will bring out its lyrical qualities, and this poem might well serve as a prologue to Marvell's "To His Coy Mistress" (pp. 495–96).

"Corinna's Going A-Maying" (pp. 492–93)
The command in line 15, "put on your foliage," condenses the theme of beauty in nature and person that runs throughout the poem. A transforma-

tion is occurring, as we see in stanza 3, where the opposition between country and city is broken down, and where, in service to this pagan ritual, houses are transformed into tabernacles.

"To His Coy Mistress" (pp. 494–96)

The syllogistic structure of this poem (if, but, therefore) has frequently been discussed. You will want to spend time on the difference in imagery and attitudes toward time in each of the three sections of the poem: the hyperboles of endless time in lines 1–20; the swift passage of human lifetime leading to the eternity of the tomb in lines 21–32; the violent imagery of seizing and devouring present time in lines 33–46. Students should consider the effect of each part of this persuasive argument on the mistress. Also, how would you characterize the speaker? Is he merely a lustful wretch with a powerful command of rhetoric? How might the woman respond to the speaker?

"The Garden" (pp. 496–98)

I would suggest teaching this poem with "To His Coy Mistress" to compare and contrast the attitudes of the two speakers. You might ask if the speaker in "The Garden" is also the speaker in "To His Coy Mistress"—but after his mistress has refused him. This garden is compared to Eden before Eve invaded it (lines 57–64). Why has the speaker withdrawn from life? Note, however, that he hasn't left passion behind, but rather that passion has been transformed into natural things (lines 25–32), and his response to such things (lines 33–40) is extremely sensual. (Would Freud call this displacement?) Much of the fun and challenge of this poem is in trying to define what "a green thought in a green shade" is.

"The Fair Singer" (p. 498)

Again, a different voice, this one perhaps more conventional than those in "To His Coy Mistress" and "The Garden" in its use of Petrarchan imagery (the war of love, the eyes that conquer). Students might compare the problem of entanglement here with being ensnared in "The Garden" and of dismantling and disentangling in "The Coronet." Or you might ask your students how they would describe the effect of their favorite singer's voice on them, so as to give them an idea of the challenge of putting a musical experience into words. Marvell succeeds admirably in lines 11–12:

> Whose subtle art invisibly can wreathe
> My fetters of the very air I breathe?

This poem can also be compared with the two versions of D. H. Lawrence's "Piano" (pp. 431–32).

"The Coronet" (pp. 498–99)

J. B. Leishman finds this "curious and arresting" poem "quite unlike any other seventeenth-century religious poem" (*The Art of Marvell's Poetry*). Leishman can't decide whether this pictorial poem "might be described as an emblematic pastoral or a pastoral emblem." Fortunately, students will be familiar with the emblematic image of Christ crowned with thorns. For the pastoral element, refer them to Herrick's "Corinna's Going A-Maying" (pp. 492–94). This poem might be discussed for its use and its rejection of pastoral conventions, the rejection suggested by the dismantling of the "fragrant tow'rs" in line 7.

Notes: line 7: "fragrant tow'rs" are high, full headdresses worn by women. Line 22: "my curious frame" is the coronet, an elaborate frame of flowers. Line 23: "these" refers to flowers.

WILLIAM BLAKE

All of the poems here except "Auguries of Innocence" are from *Songs of Experience*. You might want to bring to class an illustrated edition of *Songs of Innocence and Experience* so that students can see how the visual and verbal texts work together. The comparison of the two can be enlightening and at times amusing (or maddening) as shown in this note on "The Tyger" in Geoffrey Keyne's edition: "In some copies of the book the animal is a ferocious carnivore painted in lurid colors. In others it appears to smile as if it were a tame cat. Perhaps Blake did not intend to dispel the mystery of this poem by printing an animal of consistent or obvious character."

For Blake, innocence and experience are contrary states like heaven and hell. In *Songs of Experience,* the innocence, freedom and joy of children is cankered or silenced by adult intrusion. In an introductory class, a heavy dose of Blake's visionary philosophy isn't necessary. What is necessary is close attention to the imagery and rhythms of the poetry. These short poems may at first appear simplistic to students. To dispel that impression, you might take a close look at their metrical schemes. For an excellent discussion of Blake's metrics, see Alicia Ostriker, "Metrics: Pattern and Variation" in her *Vision and Verse in William Blake*.

"The Clod and the Pebble" (p. 500)

In this little dialogue of contrary beliefs, you might ask what the relationship between the two speakers is. The clod may be considered the voice of innocence, the pebble that of experience, but the second stanza of the poem challenges such a reductive reading. Consider the different voices ("So sung" and "Warbled out"), the different locations (road and brook), as well as the different philosophies of love. Can the clod and the pebble understand each other? Is Blake's refusal to affirm either of the philosophies in a final way satisfying? Where does it leave the reader?

"The Chimney-Sweeper" (p. 501)

What effect is created by describing the chimney-sweeper as "A little black thing"? What injury have the sweep's parents done to him? Why does he continue to dance and sing? And how can heaven be made out of misery? (You might mention that Satan offers a similar view of things in *Paradise Lost*.)

"The Sick Rose" (p. 501)

This poem has frequently been read as a sexual allegory or as an allegory of materialism (the howling storm) bringing the corrupting worm to canker earthly love (the rose). In discussing this poem, I would resist freighting it with symbolic meaning. See what connotations the students connect with rose, worm, storm, and so on. You might want to look at Michael Riffaterre's discussion of the poem and of its critics in "The Self-Sufficient Text" (*Diacritics*, Fall 1973). According to Riffaterre, "a proper reading entails no more than a knowledge of the language." You may not agree with this, but it's a theory worth testing in an introductory poetry class.

"The Tyger" (pp. 501–2)

This poem is a series of questions, none of which can be answered satisfactorily. Is the tiger created by a good force or an evil one? Are we meant to contrast the tiger with the lamb in *Songs of Innocence*? In that poem, the question "Little lamb who made thee" is answered: "He is called by thy name/ For he calls himself a lamb." Perhaps the tiger is a symbol of divine wrath, but lest class discussion lapse into personal religious opinions, you might start by paying attention to the "fearful symmetry" of the poem, and the insistent spondaic beat that urges on those questions. (A brief discussion of the metrics of this poem appears on pp. 453–54 in the "Elements of Poetry" section.) Note also how alliteration ("burning bright") contributes to the rhythm and assonance to the tone ("the fire of thine eyes").

"London" (p. 502)

This is a poem of powerful imagery which should be carefully considered before discussing the social implications of the poem and their historical context. What are manacles? What are "mind-forg'd manacles"? The chimney-sweeper's cry has been heard in "The Chimney-Sweeper," and that poem will help to explain lines 9–10.

"Auguries of Innocence" (pp. 503–5)

The first four lines should be discussed before considering the epigrammatic couplets that follow. Lines 125–26 are important for an understanding of Blake's vision: "We are led to believe a lie/ When we see not through the eye." A seeing with the soul is suggested here, as is the opposite idea of merely seeing *with* one's eyes. The Pickering manuscript shows Blake's revision of line 126: "When we see [With *del.*] not Thro' the eye."

WILLIAM WORDSWORTH

"To My Sister" (pp. 506–7)

If you are planning to teach Wordsworth's "Ode: Intimations of Immortality," you will find these earlier poems a helpful introduction.

Note the insistent tone of the first five stanzas, which are a call to seize the day, to yield oneself to nature. This poem can be compared with Herrick's "Corinna's Going A-Maying," which has a similar theme, but a quite different vision of nature. In "To My Sister" the celebration is of the circle of love emanating from the "blessed power" in nature which runs "from earth to man, from man to earth." You might begin by asking what Wordsworth means by "idleness" and what values he associates with it. What are "joyless forms"? Why does the human heart make "*silent* laws"? Comparing the values presented in this poem with those in "To His Coy Mistress" is sure to provoke discussion.

"I Wandered Lonely as a Cloud" (p. 508)

What mood does the opening simile suggest, and what change in mood occurs in this poem? For Wordsworth, the importance of seeing is paramount. To see means to experience with all one's senses and emotions. The last stanza recalls the theory of the generation of poetry set forth in Wordsworth's Preface to the *Lyrical Ballads*: "I have said that poetry is the spontaneous overflow of powerful feelings: it takes its origin from emotion recollected in tranquility: the emotion is contemplated till by a species of reaction the tranquility gradually disappears, and an emotion, kindred to that which was before the subject of contemplation, is gradually produced, and does itself actually exist in the mind." The "powerful feeling" in this poem is in part produced by the suddenness with which the speaker comes upon the daffodils ("When all at once I saw"). *How* he sees these flowers is what should be discussed here.

"Ode: Intimations of Immortality" (pp. 508–14)

The epigraph is taken from an earlier poem, "My Heart Leaps Up." "Natural piety" refers to reverence for nature. The child is a central figure in the poem, but more precisely, it is the passing of childlike vision that is the subject of the poem. In a note to the poem, Wordsworth makes this clear: "To that dreamlike vividness and splendor which invest objects of sight in childhood, every one, I believe, if he would look back, could bear testimony . . ." (I would suggest testing this statement by asking students to reflect back as far as they can to the first scene that flashes upon their "inward eyes," and writing up this episode from a child's point of view and from their present point of view.)

If you intend to tackle this poem in depth, Wordsworth's discussion of his use of the Platonic belief in the immortality and pre-existence of the soul might be helpful:

> It is far too shadowy a notion to be recommended to faith, as more than an element in our instincts of immortality. But let us bear in mind that, though the idea is not advanced in revelation, there is nothing there to contradict it, and the fall of man presents an analogy in its favor. Accordingly, a pre-existent state has entered into the popular creeds of many nations; and, among all persons acquainted with classic literature, is known as an ingredient in Platonic philosophy. Archimedes said that he could move the world if he had a point whereon to rest his machine. Who has not felt the same aspirations as regards the world of his own mind? Having to wield some of its elements when I was impelled to write this poem on the Immortality of the Soul, I took hold of the notion of pre-existence as having sufficient foundation in humanity for authorizing me to make for my purpose the best use of it I could as a poet.

If you are interested in further pursuing the Platonic background of the poem, refer to *Phaedo*, 72–76, for a discussion on knowledge as recollection.

In teaching longer poems, a useful exercise is asking students to write an abstract or precis of the poem.

TWO SONNETS

(Another of Wordsworth's sonnets, "It is a beauteous evening," can be found in the "Elements of Poetry" section, p. 435.)

4 "Earth has not anything to show more fair" (p. 514)

This sonnet is a fine example of Wordsworth's mastery of description and meditation. You might want to ask students which descriptive elements are presented objectively and which subjectively. Is it paradoxical to describe this sight as "so touching in its majesty"? How is the simile "like a garment" developed? What is the effect of personification in the poem? What does such personification suggest about the speaker's attitude toward an awakened London?

14 "The world is too much with us . . ." (pp. 514–15)

How would you describe the stance of the speaker in the octave of this sonnet? (Some students have suggested that *he* is certainly "out of tune".) What does it mean to be "out of tune"? The poem turns sharply in the middle of line 9 with the exclamation, "Great God!" How does the new imagery introduced here complicate or develop the material presented in the octave?

29 "Bright Star" (p. 515)

Regarding the sestet of this sonnet, H. W. Garrod asks, "But what has the Bright Star got to do with any of it? The poet asks of the star only steadfastness and unchangeability. But do they really matter to him? Does the Bright Star really stand for anything in which the sonnet culminates?" (from notes to "Bright Star" in *Keats: Poetical Works*). Your students may well ask the same questions. In the octave, the speaker both defines and rejects the star's steadfast qualities. The sestet then defines the speaker's concept of steadfastness. Where the star is personified as an eternal, sleepless Hermit watching over earth's movements, the speaker, longing for the same immortality, rejects such an isolated, eremitic steadfastness. His is a lover's steadfastness where nearness is all. He too will be awake forever, but instead of watching, as the star does, other senses are more involved, such as touching and hearing.

"On the Sonnet" (p. 516)

Keats's concern with developing new forms for English poetry is expressed in a letter to George and Georgiana Keats (April 30, 1819): "I have been endeavouring to discover a better Sonnet stanza than we have. The legitimate does not suit the language over-well from the pouncing rhymes—the other kind appears too elegiac—and the couplet at the end of it has seldom a pleasing effect—I do not pretend to have succeeded—it will explain itself."

Compare the structure and rhyme scheme of this sonnet with that of "Bright Star," which has the Petrarchan structure of Shakespeare's sonnets.

"Ode to a Nightingale" (pp. 516–18)

Keats's five Great Odes were all written between April and September, 1819. The first draft of this Ode was supposedly written as Keats actually listened to a nightingale singing on a day in May.

Rather than glaze students' eyes with a lecture on Keats's "yearning and fondness . . . for the beautiful," it will be more useful to work through the development of the mood in this poem: the entrance into the song which begins to induce a state of dreaminess, the move to a closeness with "easeful Death," the comparison between death and immortality, the waking out of the dream state. The human state is to be "born for death," a realization which gives poignancy to our lives, and which heightens our imaginative powers. This theme is taken up in Wallace Stevens's "Sunday Morning" (pp. 575–78). Also, for its description of the state of waking-sleeping, compare Robert Frost's "After Apple-picking" (pp. 570–71). You might also ask whether the speaker in "Stopping by Woods on a Snowy Evening" (p. 571) is "half in love with easeful Death."

"Ode on a Grecian Urn" (pp. 518–20)

If your students find the last two lines puzzling, they should; few critics of the poem agree on their meaning. Interpretation is complicated by the fact that while the first edition of the poem in 1820 has quotation marks around "beauty is truth, truth beauty," other editions do not. Are the last two lines spoken by the Urn? And is the "Beauty is truth" statement very profound or very silly? Such a controversy introduces an opportunity to remind students to read poetry carefully and closely. What evidence does the poem provide for an interpretation of those concluding lines?

The poem is structured as a "reading" of the urn, but it's certainly not an objective reading, for this urn existed only in Keats's imagination, though scenes similar to those he describes can be found on Grecian amphorae and friezes. What is the speaker's attitude toward the urn? Why does he call it "Sylvan historian"? And why, in the final stanza, is it referred to as "Cold Pastoral"?

Compare: Sylvia Plath, "Edge" (p. 661)

"Ode to Autumn" (pp. 520–21)

The serenity of the "more thoughtful and quiet power" felt by Keats when he wrote this Ode in mid-September 1819 is evident in its mood. Certainly the effects produced by alliteration and assonance (in its softest tones) should be studied here. The three stanzas of the poem present three stages of autumn: ripeness, the last harvest of fruits and flowers; the harvest itself with autumn personified as harvester; the singular music of later autumn. How would you describe this music of autumn? (You might ask students to change the language of the last stanza to suggest "the songs of Spring.") Compare the tone of the last stanza with that of the last stanza of Wallace Stevens's "Sunday Morning," written about one hundred years after "Ode to Autumn."

ALFRED, LORD TENNYSON

"Ulysses" (pp. 522–23)

You may want to refer your students to the discussion of the dramatic monologue in the "Elements of Poetry" section, pp. 427–32.

This poem has been the subject of a variety of readings, in part because the sources Tennyson gives for "Ulysses" present conflicting versions of Ulysses: Homer's *Odyssey*, xi, 100–137, and Dante's *Inferno*, xxvi, 90ff. In the *Odyssey*, Tiresias predicts that after Ulysses has come home and "slain the wooers in thy halls," he will go forth on another voyage, and eventually die of "sleek old age, and thy people shall dwell in prosperity around thee." Dante's Ulysses was consumed by an overwhelming zeal to explore the world, which resulted in a last, fatal voyage beyond "bound'ries not to be o'erstepped by man." He has persuaded his elderly crew to follow him:

Ye were not form'd to live the life of brutes,
But virtue to pursue and knowledge high.

Further, "Ulysses" was written in 1833, shortly after the death of Tennyson's beloved friend, Henry Hallam. Tennyson commented that the poem "gives the feeling about the need of going forward and braving the struggle of life perhaps more simply than anything in *In Memoriam.*"

First, the audience in the poem should be considered. Ulysses is addressing both his followers, the crew who will go with him on his voyage, and a larger audience, to whom he presents his son Telemachus, who will inherit rule over the Ithacans. Lines 1–32 present Ulysses's present state and his desire to travel. For line 4, "Unequal laws unto a savage race," Tennyson has provided this note: "Not 'unjust,' but 'not affecting all in the same manner or degree,' a primitive state of law consequent upon the Ithacans being a 'savage race.' " Lines 33–43: Ulysses presents Telemachus. What relationship between the two is suggested by "He works his work, I mine"? Lines 44–70: Ulysses's persuasive rhetoric is directed to his crew, to inspire them for a final "work of noble note" before "Death closes all."

The main questions are "Should Ulysses be considered a responsible or irresponsible person?" and "Is the journey which he plans to take a negative or positive venture?" If you are interested in the Victorian background to this poem, see the section on "Aspiration without an Object," in Walter Houghton's *The Victorian Frame of Mind.*

"The Eagle" (p. 523)

The imagery in this poem should certainly be compared with that in Whitman's "The Dalliance of the Eagles" (p. 541). Whitman's eagles are directly observed, while Tennyson's eagle might be described as a product of the imagination. Some critics have objected to an eagle with hands, saying that Tennyson preferred hands to claws for the sake of his rhyme scheme. This might be a good opportunity to test that assumption and introduce students to the problems of meter and rhyme. Ask them to rewrite the first stanza, giving the eagle "claws" rather than "hands."

"Tears, Idle Tears" (p. 524)

According to Tennyson, "This song came to me on the yellowing autumn-tide at Tintern Abbey, full for me of its bygone memories." Further, Tennyson claims the poem is not about real woe, "it was rather the yearning that young people occasionally experience for that which seems to have passed away from them forever." Students are usually surprised that this poem presents a *young* person's mood.

How is the opening statement, "I know not what they mean," developed? Are we ever told specifically the cause of these tears? Why are they called "idle tears"? What effect does the repetition of the last line of each stanza produce?

Compare: Gerard Manley Hopkins, "Spring and Fall" (p. 550)

From "In Memoriam" (pp. 524–26)

You may want to teach one or more of these selections with other elegies in the anthology, asking students to consider whether a particular poem is more about the person who died or the grief of the living person. A comparison of imagery, especially natural imagery, will also be useful. Some suggestions for comparison:

W. H. Auden, "In Memory of W. B. Yeats" (pp. 615–16)
Theodore Roethke, "Elegy for Jane" (pp. 619–20)
Dylan Thomas, "A Refusal to Mourn the Death, by Fire, of a Child . . ." (pp. 623–24)
W. S. Merwin, "Elegy" (p. 639)
Philip Levine, "Ricky" (pp. 644–47)

You might also ask students whether E. E. Cummings's "Buffalo Bill's" (pp. 604–5) and Gwendolyn Brooks's "The Rites for Cousin Vit" (p. 633) can be considered elegies.

7 "Dark house, by which once more I stand" (p. 524)

This relatively uncomplicated poem provides a good opportunity to study figurative language. Ask students to consider the "dark house" and the "doors" on the denotative level, the connotative level, and in the context of the poem. Why does the speaker describe himself as "a guilty thing"? What effect is produced by the monosyllabic words and the alliteration in the last line?

8 "A happy lover . . ." (p. 525)

This poem should be compared with "Dark house" with respect to dark-light opposition and use of house imagery. Note that the speaker's gift of poetry is brought to yet another house: the tomb.

115 "Now fades the last long streak . . ." (pp. 525–26)

What place does spring have in an elegiac poem? Compare this poem with the two previous ones. What change has taken place in the speaker?

ROBERT BROWNING

"Soliloquy of the Spanish Cloister" (pp. 527–29)

Refer students to the "Drama and Narration" section in the "Elements of Poetry" section, pp. 428–29, for a discussion of an excerpt from Browning's "Fra Lippo Lippi," and for approaches to the dramatic monologue.

Certainly, a malicious and witty personality is revealed in the speaker of "Soliloquy," but we should also consider Brother Lawrence, and why he elicits such a reaction from the speaker. For a writing assignment, ask students to write a brief soliloquy with Brother Lawrence as speaker.

"My Last Duchess" (pp. 529–30)

The direful implications of line 2, "Looking as if she were alive," which merely suggests a life-like portrait, are not fully evident until lines 46–47: "There she stands/ As if alive." And why is the portrait covered with a curtain? Be sure students know who is speaking and who the audience in the poem is: an envoy from a Count whose daughter is to marry the Duke. Full realization that the dowry of the *next* wife is being discussed after the Duke has calmly described why he had his *last* wife put away (and were there more before her?) helps students realize how smoothly amoral the Duke is. You may find you need to place the poem in the context of Italian Renaissance manners and morals. The Duke is a collector, a connoisseur of art, as his references to Fra Pandolf and Claus of Innsbruck (and the painting itself) suggest. How might this interest affect his attitude toward life? And specifically, toward his late wife?

"The Bishop Orders His Tomb . . ." (pp. 530–33)

John Ruskin found this poem a masterly evocation "of the Renaissance spirit—its worldliness, inconsistency, pride, hypocrisy, ignorance of itself, love of art, of luxury, and of good Latin."

Consider the first line of the poem, "Vanity, saith the preacher, vanity!" (Ecclesiastes 1:2). How is the theme of vanity developed throughout the poem? Will the sons follow their father's instructions? Where in the poem are there indications that they may not?

Note: line 3: "Nephews" is a euphemism for illegitimate sons.

Some other dramatic monologues that might be compared with Browning's are:

Alfred, Lord Tennyson, "Ulysses" (pp. 522–23)

T. S. Eliot, "The Love Song of J. Alfred Prufrock" (pp. 595–99)

Robert Lowell, "Skunk Hour" (pp. 627–28)

"The Lost Mistress" (pp. 533–34)

What images in the poem suggest loss, or the ending of an affair? Does the speaker really believe "All's over"?

Compare: W. S. Merwin, "When You Go Away" (p. 639)

WALT WHITMAN

"Poets to Come" (p. 535)

This poem can be read as a short introduction to "Crossing Brooklyn Ferry." In Whitman's poetry, the reader is directly addressed, and asked to become involved. In his 1855 Preface to *Leaves of Grass*, Whitman explains the reader's task:

> . . . the process of reading is not a half-sleep, but, in the highest
> sense, an exercise, a gymnast's struggle; that the reader is to do
> something for himself, must be on the alert, must himself or
> herself construct indeed the poem, argument, history, metaphysi-
> cal essay—the text furnishing the hints, the clue, the start or
> frame-work.

This is of course good advice for reading anything. But Whitman is striving for immortality through poetry in a transcendental sense, through his readers: "Not today is to justify me and answer what I am for . . . you must justify me." In one sense, he means the progress of a democratic society; that we will fulfill the ideals of democracy in which he believed. Poets of today must continue to sing Whitman's song of America, and continue to define the human experience. You might point out to students that most American poets were influenced by Whitman, either rebelling against his verbosity, like the early Ezra Pound, or answering his call, like William Carlos Williams, or even directly imitating his style, like Allen Ginsberg.

"Crossing Brooklyn Ferry" (pp. 535–40)
Consider the location of the speaker in the poem, and his relation to the movement of time—present, past, future—in the poem. Is the poem spe-cifically about the ferry ride between Brooklyn and Manhattan, or is it about other journeys as well? In what parts of the poem does Whitman use catalogues of specific details? Why?

Note that in line 126, "dumb beautiful ministers" refers to the "objects" of line 125. Material things are called "ministers" because the material here is seen as symbolic of the spiritual. Twice, in sections 3 and 9, "spokes of light" around "my head, or any one's head" appear. Students may be quick to point out these reflections as Christ-images. Perhaps Whitman means to suggest that we are all Christlike, that there is divinity in all of us. But this is a poem of *becoming,* of life and things of this life in flux, moving toward eternity. For Whitman, the bodily senses are as important as the spiritual: "What gods can exceed these that clasp me by the hand . . . ?"

"I Hear America Singing" (p. 540)
This poem needs little explanation; it can serve as a small example of Whitman's catalogue approach to experience. The singing presumes that workers are proud and happy with what they do, and that the song of each is an *individual* one, as Whitman makes clear in "Crossing Brooklyn Ferry." He believes in individual identity—the special qualities of each person—but sees individuals as parts of a whole, a spiritual unity.

"The World below the Brine" (pp. 540–41)
This poem is from the "Sea-Drift" section of *Leaves of Grass,* a section which starts with the magnificent "Out of the Cradle Endlessly Rocking." In this little poem, the world above the brine is a reflection of the world

below it, a world from which man has evolved into his present world. As the last line makes clear, the world above the brine is seen as another step in upward evolution.

"The Dalliance of the Eagles" (p. 541)
(See the discussion of Tennyson's "The Eagle" on p. 59 of this manual.) This poem is from the "By the Roadside" section of *Leaves of Grass*, and appears as one of a series of descriptions and meditations. Why is this meeting described as a "dalliance"? Note how description of the birds moves back and forth from a sense of two things yet one thing, until the final parting.

"A Sight in Camp in the Daybreak Gray and Dim" (pp. 541–42)
This poem is from "Drum-Taps," a group of Civil War poems. Students should consider the meaning of the "blanket covering all," and what is suggested about the removal of that blanket. What statement is made about war in this poem?

"Who Learns My Lesson Complete?" (pp. 542–43)
This poem is from the "Autumn Rivulets" section of *Leaves of Grass*. Why does the speaker say his lesson is "no lesson—it lets down the bars to a good lesson . . ."? Define "wonderful" in the context of this poem. Does the repetition of this word strengthen the poem or weaken it?
   Note: line 7: "effuse" means to pour out.

"The Ox-Tamer" (p. 543)
This poem is also from "Autumn Rivulets." Whitman refers to the poem as "my recitative," which refers not so much to recitation as it does to music. Recitative is a style used in opera "in which the text is declaimed in the rhythm of natural speech" (*American Heritage Dictionary*.) Whitman's poetry was influenced by his love of opera. If you have any musical students, you might ask them to "declaim" this poem.
   What effect does the repetition of "See you" and "see" have in this poem? What is the speaker's relationship with the ox-tamer? (Note especially lines 17–18.)

"As I Sit Writing Here" (p. 544)
This is a late poem from "Sands at Seventy." Consider the effect of the inverted word order in line 2: "Not my least burden is . . ." What attitude toward life (and art) is expressed in such figurative speech as "Ungracious glooms" and "Whimpering *ennui*"?

EMILY DICKINSON

Because Dickinson's poems look so simple and unintimidating at first glance, they are especially useful for writing assignments done before class discussion (and we all know that class discussion goes better *after* students have written on something). You can assign a response paper or a paper on imagery in one of the poems. Or, because the poems are so syntactically compressed, you might ask students to write paraphrases of them.

"Success Is Counted Sweetest" (pp. 544–45)
The poem develops out of the first two epigrammatic lines. Why *"purple host"?* How many points of view are present in the last lines?

"I Never Hear the Word . . ." (p. 545)
What sorts of escape are being discussed here? How might you describe the speaker's situation in this poem?

"I'm 'Wife'—I've Finished That" (p. 545)
What is the relationship between "Czar" and "Woman"? And why are "Wife" and "woman" in quotation marks? What attitude towards marriage is suggested by "soft eclipse"? Consider the comparison in stanza 2 between Girl-Woman and Earth-Heaven, and the comparison in stanza 3 between "This . . . comfort" and "That . . . pain." Try to define the two states. Why does the speaker not wish to compare them? And why the imperative ending: "Stop there!"?

"What Is—'Paradise' " (pp. 545–46)
The speaker in this poem sounds (deceptively) like a child. What does the use of a child-persona allow the poet to do? In what terms is Paradise being defined? A discussion of irony would be appropriate here, because of the danger of students reading this poem as a piece of Victorian sentimentality.

Note, line 16: "Ransomed folks" are the elect, those who are sure they are going to heaven.

"I Heard a Fly Buzz . . ." (p. 546)
This is a remarkable poem, describing the last moment before death—but where is the speaker located? The fly brings this moment of death down to a homely level, and that "Blue—uncertain stumbling Buzz" will give you a chance to discuss synesthesia if you wish. You might ask which "King" is referred to in lines 7–8.

"The Heart Asks Pleasure—First" (pp. 546–47)
What does the progression in the poem suggest about its possible meaning? What does "Excuse from Pain" mean? What would be an example of one of "those little Anodynes / That deaden suffering"? Who or what is the heart's "Inquisitor"?

"Because I Could Not Stop for Death" (p. 547)
How is Death characterized in the poem? What is the tone of the first three stanzas? What change takes place at the beginning of the fourth stanza? What attitude toward dying is suggested by the poem?

"A Narrow Fellow in the Grass" (pp. 547–48)
Who ever thinks of a snake as a "fellow"? What effect is gained by the use of this term? How much of the poem is about the movements of the snake, and how much about the effect on the observer of those movements? What do the tension and chill of the last lines suggest? Why does the snake cause such a feeling?

Compare: Marianne Moore, "The Fish" (pp. 591–92) and "A Jellyfish" (pp. 592–93)

GERARD MANLEY HOPKINS

"God's Grandeur" (p. 549)
Hopkins's is a poetry of sound, so it is essential that students hear these poems read aloud. You might follow Hopkins's own suggestion: "To be read . . . slowly, strongly marking the rhythms and fetching out the syllables." There are two contrasting ideas in the octave of the sonnet. The first concerns "knowing how to touch" the world to reveal God's grandeur; the second comments on man's usual day-to-day existence and the resulting numbness and encrustation of material life, summed up as "nor can foot feel, being shod." Consider how rhythm, repetition, alliteration and assonance work to produce these two contrasting effects. Then consider how the different tone of the sestet is produced. This section is more meditative, but with revelatory moments of awe springing out with "Oh" and "ah!"

"The Windhover" (p. 549)
One can read the windhover as a symbol of Christ, with the physical graces of the bird analogous to the spiritual grace possible to man through Christ. Certainly the dedication "To Christ Our Lord" suggests such an analogy, but I wouldn't force it. Let the language of the poem work for itself. "Buckle" has posed a number of interpretive problems: are things in line 9 buckled on as a knight would buckle on armor, or do these qualities bend, collapse, break, as Christ's body did on the cross? Consider the effect of "blue-bleak" as opposed to "blue-black" embers. How does the structure of this sonnet compare with that of "God's Grandeur"?

"Pied Beauty" (p. 550)
This is a little hymn in praise of variety in nature. You might ask what line 10 has to do with all that's come before.

"Spring and Fall . . ." (p. 550)

Line 8, "Though worlds of wanwood leafmeal lie," was originally written as "Though forests low and leafmeal lie." You might ask students what has been gained (or lost) in this revision. Also, what are the connotations of "Goldengrove" in the context of the entire poem? And why the imperative, "And yet you *will* weep and know why"? "Ghost" here is the spirit foreseeing, knowing through sensory experience; the falling leaves turning to leafmeal predict the condition of the body after death. Margaret has had her moment of recognition.

"Thou Art Indeed Just, Lord" (pp. 550–51)

You might compare the voice of the speaker here with that of Donne in the excerpt from Devotion 19 and in the Holy Sonnets. What is the argument of the poem? What does "Time's eunuch" mean? How does this metaphor connect with the theme of growing-prospering and infertility-spending in the poem?

Note: line 11: "fretty chervil" is cow-parsley, a plant with serrated, lacy leaves.

A. E. HOUSMAN

(Note: another Housman poem, "With rue my heart is laden," appears in the "Elements of Poetry" section, pp. 455–56, with a discussion of its metrics.)

2 "Loveliest of trees . . ." (pp. 551–52)

This little lyric is of the *carpe diem* school, but its argument has a gentler tone than most such poems. This is a good place to consider metaphor: "To see the cherry hung with snow." Why snow? Its literal meaning is antithetical to the season of Eastertide, but visually it works (blossoms white as snow). What connotations are connected with snow? How does this metaphor contribute to the meaning of the poem?

13 "When I was one-and-twenty" (p. 552)

The metrics of this poem should be closely considered. How does Housman vary the meter to keep the poem from falling into a sing-song pattern?

19 "The time you won . . ." (pp. 552–53)

With this poem, you might explore with your students the way in which the rhyme scheme here tightens the argument of the poem. Discuss how the poem is structured around two races, both of which the youth is considered to have won. In the last line, we assume that a girl's garland would be of roses, so you might discuss the metaphoric use of the laurel and the rose. Can this poem be considered an elegy? Or does the ironic stance of the narrator preclude that?

27 "Is my team ploughing?" (pp. 553–54)

This poem has its roots in the early ballad form: compare its supernatural theme with "The Unquiet Grave," its question and answer structure with "The Demon Lover" and "Edward," and its surprise ending with "Edward." How is repetition used to create a dramatic effect in the poem?

62 "Terence, this is stupid stuff" (pp. 554–56)

Terence was a Roman satiric poet, and Housman's original title for *A Shropshire Lad* was *The Poems of Terence Hearsay*. The first 14 lines of the poem are a comedy-parody of Housman's own poetry. The rest of the poem is a reply. What is Terence accused of, and how does his defense make a case for the examples of Housman's poetry in this anthology? In line 18, the answer to the question is: to use Trent River water in Burton's breweries. If your students are familiar with *Paradise Lost,* you might ask for comments on lines 21–22, or you might read them the opening lines of *Paradise Lost.* Lines 59–76 are a retelling of the story of Mithridates, King of Pontus (d. 63 B.C.), who achieved immunity to poison by taking gradually increased doses of it. How do these lines support Terence's defense of poetry?

"Eight O'Clock" (p. 556)

This is an excellent poem for discussion of metrics and patterns of alliteration. First, make sure students understand the position of the "He" in the poem. What are the two attitudes toward time presented here? And how do the metrics and alliteration underscore those attitudes?

Compare: W. H. Auden, "As I Walked Out One Evening" (pp. 611–13)

WILLIAM BUTLER YEATS

(Another Yeats poem, "The Dolls," appears in the discussion of the symbol in the "Elements of Poetry" section, p. 441.)

"The Lake Isle of Innisfree" (p. 557)

You might want to contrast the music of this poem—its alliteration, assonance, and diction—with Housman's "Eight O'Clock."

In his *Autobiography,* Yeats recalled the creation of the poem:

> I had still the ambition, formed in Sligo in my teens, of living in imitation of Thoreau on Innisfree, a little island in Lough Gill, and when walking through Fleet Street [London] very homesick I heard a little tinkle of water and saw a fountain in a shop-window which balanced a little ball upon its jet, and began to remember lake water. From the sudden remembrance came my poem *Innisfree,* my first lyric with anything in its rhythm of my own music.

The crystallization of Yeats's general feeling of homesickness results from a particular sound. For a writing assignment, you might ask students to describe what sight, sound, or smell induces in them a feeling of home-sickness or desire for a special place of escape.

"The Song of Wandering Aengus" (pp. 557–58)

An example of Yeats's early preoccupation with fantasy and fairy tale, the theme of this poem is explained by Yeats: "The Tribes of the goddess Danu can take all shapes, and those that are in the waters take often the shapes of fish." The demonic qualities of such spirits and their effect on poets are thoroughly discussed by Robert Graves in *The White Goddess*.

"The Wild Swans at Coole" (pp. 558–59)

I have always been interested in the number problem here: if there are 59 swans, only 58 of them can paddle "lover by lover." Is the poet the 60th lover, if only temporarily? What does it mean to be able to count the swans? Note the different images in stanzas 1 and 2, for a start, and then the movement from "great broken rings" in stanza 2 to the image of classical perfection in the final stanza. You may want to compare Yeats's view of nature with Wordsworth's.

Notes: Coole Park, in western Ireland, was the estate of Yeats's friend and patroness, Lady Gregory. Lines 7–8: The poem was written in 1916; Yeats had first visited Coole Park in 1897.

"The Fisherman" (pp. 559–60)

This is a poem about poetry, and more specifically, Yeats's view of his poetry. Who are the two audiences mentioned in the poem? What is the poet's relationship with each? Why does he scorn one of these audiences? What is meant by a poem that is "cold/ And passionate as the dawn"?

"Leda and the Swan" (p. 560)

From whose point of view is the action described? There are Christian parallels in the poem, and discussing might help to answer the final question about knowledge and power. Though Yeats was in a political mood when he started the poem, thinking change in history was possible only if there were "some movement from above preceded by some violent an-nunciation," he found that as he wrote, "bird and lady took such posses-sion of the scene that all politics went out of it."

"Sailing to Byzantium" (pp. 560–61)

This poem may be approached in context with the other Yeats poems in the anthology, if you are concentrating on the development of Yeats's poetry. If you wish to use "Sailing to Byzantium" as an example of how a poem gets made, see Chapter V of Jon Stallworthy's *Between the Lines*, where Yeats's revisions are presented and discussed. This is an excellent way to open up the poem, for students are fascinated with the revelation of the poetic process. For Yeats's use of symbols—which he differentiates from metaphors—see his essay, "The Symbolism of Poetry," in *Essays and Introductions*. For Yeats's use of mythology in this poem and in "Leda and the Swan," see "Book V: Dove or Swan" in Yeats's *A Vision*. From that essay, here are Yeats's thoughts on Byzantium:

> I think that in early Byzantium, maybe never before or since in recorded history, religious, aesthetic and practical life were one, that architect and artificers—though not, it may be, poets, for language had been the instrument of controversy and must have grown abstract—spoke to the multitude and the few alike, the painter, the mosaic worker in gold and silver, the illuminator of sacred books, were almost impersonal, almost perhaps without the consciousness of individual design, absorbed in their subject matter and that the vision of a whole people.

I would not recommend a heavy dose of Yeats's mythological and historical beliefs for introductory students—unless, of course, they ask for it. The development of patterns of imagery, connected to the contrasts of mortality ("Those dying generations") and immortality ("Monuments of unaging intellect") should be worked through carefully.

Compare: John Keats, "Ode to a Nightingale" and "Ode on a Grecian Urn"
W. B. Yeats, "After Long Silence" and "The Circus Animals' Desertion"
Wallace Stevens, "Sunday Morning"

"For Anne Gregory" (pp. 561–62)
Note the oppositions at work in the poem: soul versus bodily appearance, "young men in despair" versus "old religious man," and the speaker and the young woman. How would you characterize the speaker in the first and third stanzas?

"After Long Silence" (p. 562)
In this poem there are also oppositions between youth and age, ignorance and wisdom. What speech is possible? Why is it described as "descant"? Why has there been "long silence"?

"The Circus Animals' Desertion" (pp. 562–63)
In this late poem (1939), Yeats's early themes are described as "circus animals" on parade, and they are contrasted with his later themes from the heart: life versus art, reality versus unreality are introduced in part I. Consider here the implied image of poet as ringmaster. In part II, Yeats's earlier themes are presented as "dreams," but though they are also written from the heart, art has tended to dominate life (lines 32–33). Part III: students may read this section as a negative statement, but is it really? What does it mean to return to the place "where all ladders start"? Remind students that some of Yeats's greatest poetry (such as this poem) was

written in old age (Wallace Stevens is another poet who improved with age). If you and your students have worked with Wordsworth's "Ode: Intimations of Immortality," you might compare Wordsworth's qualified praise of "years that bring the philosophic mind" with Yeats's view of the latter part of life. I leave it to you to say what you will about the poetry of Wordsworth's old age.

Notes: line 10: Oisin (pronounced "Usheen") was led by the fairy Niam (pronounced "Nee-ave") to the three islands referred to in line 12. *Wanderings of Oisin* (1889) was Yeats's first important long work. Lines 18–20: In Yeats's first play, *The Countess Cathleen* (1892), Countess Cathleen sells her soul to the devil to save the souls of her starving countrymen. She eventually is saved. Line 21: "my dear" refers to Maud Gonne, an actress and an activist for Irish liberation with whom Yeats was in love. Yeats wrote *The Countess Cathleen* for Maud Gonne. Lines 25–26: A reference to an early play, *On Baile's Strand* (1903), in which Cuchulain (pronounced "Cuhoolin"), in a fit of madness after learning he has killed his own son, goes out to fight the waves. While people run out to watch, the Fool and the Blind Man go off to steal the bread from their ovens.

EDWIN ARLINGTON ROBINSON

(Another of Robinson's poems, "Reuben Bright," may be found in the "Elements of Poetry" section, pp. 430–31, with a discussion of its narrative elements.)

"Richard Cory" (pp. 564–65)

Cory is described as "always human," but what do such words as "crown," "imperially," "glittered" and "king" suggest about the way he is perceived by his townspeople? The use of connectives—and, but, so—at the beginning of many of the lines is worth noting. What effect does such syntax have on the tone of the poem? Students might like to hear Paul Simon's version of "Richard Cory," a retelling of the poem which expands the townspeople's point of view. "Richard Cory" was recorded for the album, *Sounds of Silence.*

"The Pity of the Leaves" (p. 565)

Condensed into this sonnet is a New England tragedy, the details of which are left to the imagination. We see the end of a history here: an old man in an old house living with some guilt from the past. How is the animation of nature used in the poem? How many different sounds are described in the poem? What is their cumulative effect?

"Eros Turannos" (pp. 565–66)

This poem presents another New England drama. The title is Greek for "Love the tyrant," and Eros, the god of love, is the god referred to in the last stanza of the poem. This poem has a downward movement towards that ominous last line, "Where down the blind are driven." Beginning with the image of the "engaging mask" in the first stanza, what other suggestions are there of the loss of or obscuring of vision? In stanza 5, what comments does the narrator make about the story he is presenting? What part does the town play in this drama? You might have students write a paraphrase of the "lovers" and their relationship as it is presented in the first four stanzas of the poem.

"Mr. Flood's Party" (pp. 566–68)

While it should be obvious to students that this is more than just a comic poem about the town drunk, you may wish to pay careful attention to the mixture of heroic and maternal imagery in the third and fourth stanzas to help dispel any misconceptions. How does the implied certainty of the jug (lines 29–30) as compared with "the uncertain lives of men" help to develop the meaning of "knowing that most things break"? You might present Robert Frost's comment on this poem for class discussion: "The guarded pathos of 'Mr. Flood's Party' is what makes it merciless."

Notes: lines 11–13: The poet referred to is Omar Khayyam. The seventh stanza of *The Rubaiyat* is recalled by Mr. Flood:

> Come, fill the Cup, and in the Fire of Spring
> Your Winter-garment of Repentance fling;
> The Bird of Time has but a little way
> To flutter—and the Bird is on the Wing.

Line 20: Roland, in the 8th century battle of Roncesvalles, was unwilling to blow his horn summoning help from Charlemagne until it was too late.

ROBERT FROST

"Mending Wall" (pp. 569–70)

The first line of the poem may delude the unwary student into a simplistic reading of this poem: Robert Frost doesn't like walls. Well, if the narrator doesn't approve of walls, why does he participate in the ritual of mending them every spring? Consider the relationship of the two neighbors and what their dialogue reveals about their attitudes toward walls. Consider Louis Untermeyer's comment: "The strength of 'Mending Wall' . . . rests upon a contradiction. Its two most famous lines oppose each other . . . The contradiction is logical, for the opposing statements are uttered by two different types of people—and both are right." The poem can be read as a statement about our need for boundaries and about our resentment against boundaries.

"After Apple-picking" (pp. 570–71)

This poem can be read as a realistic description of apple-picking and its physical effects because of the sensual descriptions, but its real fascination (and ambiguity) derives from the waking-dream state it evokes. Consider the entrance into the poem: what effect does the word "essence" produce? How does the breaking of the time sequence contribute to the dream-state? Note especially lines 8–17. Is the poem also a commentary on human labor in a post-lapsarian sense?

"Stopping by Woods on a Snowy Evening" (p. 571)

Most students will be familiar with this poem, and if asked what it's about, many will reply, "the death-wish," as if they had found a serious flaw in Frost's psychological makeup. You might suggest that the desire for escape from responsibilities is a natural one, and see where that takes you. Or consider the poem as a mood piece. What is the tone of the poem? How do the horse's movements contribute to the expression of this mood? Note the change in rhyme scheme in the last stanza. What effect does this change produce?

"Two Tramps in Mud Time" (pp. 571–74)

Frost's alternate title for this poem was "or, A Full-Time Interest." Frost's own philosophy about work is spelled out in the last two stanzas, and of course this attitude applies both to chopping wood and to writing poetry. Note the use of direct address in stanza 3. This provides an opportunity for you to discuss how Frost involves the reader in the poem.

"Design" (p. 574)

This fine sonnet has been described by Randall Jarrell as "The most awful of Frost's smaller poems," meaning awful in the sense of being profoundly impressive. Just so is Jarrell's reading of this poem, which can be found in his essay "To the Laodiceans" in *Poetry and the Age*. Trace the connotations of innocence and evil, starting with the first line and the diabolical mixture of a spider described as a baby: "dimpled . . . fat and white." Well, not quite like a baby; one expects babies to be pink. What does "design of darkness" mean?

   Note: lines 9–10: The heal-all is usually blue.

"Provide, Provide" (p. 574)

For me, the word "provide" conjures up the syrupy demeanor of an insurance salesman telling me to plan ahead and "provide" for my dotage. The voice here is quite different. The tone is strong, terse, and the message— cynical, perhaps? Consider how the rhyme scheme contributes to that tone, and how the opening image of Abishag dominates the poem. How might the speaker reply to an insurance salesman or to the Social Security Administration?

"The Silken Tent" (pp. 574–75)

This sonnet, originally titled "In Praise of Your Poise," was written for Frost's secretary, Kay Morrison. The sonnet is Shakespearean, and is one sentence with no breaks. If you are interested in syntactical analysis, this is a fine poem to work with, for the syntax here is as supple and elastic as the silken tent itself. Here too is a splendid example of the conceit. What does "bondage" mean in this poem? Is it opposed to freedom?

WALLACE STEVENS
"Sunday Morning" (pp. 575–78)
This poem is a meditation, presented in the form of a dialogue between the speaker of the poem and a woman who might well be considered an alter ego of the speaker. As in most Stevens poems, abstract ideas are being discussed, such as belief in a god, immortality, heaven, death, and so on. The beauty of the poem lies in the way these abstractions are made flesh. For example, in stanza 2, nature is evoked by "comforts of the sun . . . pungent fruit . . . bright, green wings." What kind of relationship with nature is suggested by "passions *of* rain"?

Notes: line 74: "disregarded plate." Stevens explained this term in a letter to Harriet Monroe: "Plate is used in the sense of so-called family plate. Disregarded refers to the disuse into which things fall that have been possessed for a long time." Line 105: "Life is as fugitive as dew upon the feet of men dancing in dew." (Stevens's gloss on this line in a letter to L. W. Payne, Jr.)

Compare: John Keats, "Ode on a Grecian Urn" (pp. 519–20) and "To Autumn" (pp. 520–21)

"Anecdote of the Jar" (p. 579)
This is a delightful expression of the art versus nature question. What does the jar look like? ("of a port" is problematical. My paraphrase is "of an imposing demeanor," which seems to go with "tall.") Why place the jar in Tennessee? Why not Arizona or New Jersey? Was the wilderness seen as "slovenly" *before* the jar was placed there?

"Thirteen Ways of Looking at a Blackbird" (pp. 579–81)
Like the preceding poem, this one is about imaginative perception, and is also, in Joseph Riddell's words, "an epistemological tour de force" (*The Clairvoyant Eye*). I suggest working through the condensed little stanzas in class, considering each image presented, and considering the different moods presented. For example, according to Stevens, stanza 13 is meant to symbolize "despair." You might also look at Ronald Sukenick's interpretation of the poem in *Wallace Stevens: Musing the Obscure*. But beware of any "one right reading" approach; this is a very fluid poem. You might ask students to attempt their own poems (or drawings) on five or six ways of looking at a duck, a leaf, a pigeon, a brother.

"The Snow Man" (p. 581)
Consider the connotations of "snow man": childhood, winter, fun, etc. But a snow man is more snow than man, especially in this poem. While

this is a poem of pure abstraction, it creates the reality of the nothing that is there through sensory information. The "nothing that is not there" might be considered as that which the imagination would provide. The poem defines "a mind of winter" through its images. To help explain lines 6–9, you might want to return to E. A. Robinson's poem "The Pity of the Leaves," where there *is* "misery in the sound of the wind." In that poem, we "see" the wind not as the wind really is but as it is interpreted through one person's imagination. In Stevens's poem, we are asked to hear the wind as the wind itself: a pure abstraction.

"A High-Toned Old Christian Woman" (pp. 581–82)

How would you describe the voice addressing the woman? The mixture of diction in the poem is worth careful attention; it's both comic ("tink and tank") and formal ("disaffected flagellants"). Two structures are mentioned: a nave and a peristyle. How do they differ in an architectural sense? How do they differ in the context of the poem? And what about the palms associated with each structure?

"Of Modern Poetry" (pp. 582–83)

You might consider using this poem as an introduction to other Stevens poems. Here we find the unique problem of modern poetry: finding "what will suffice" in place of the conventional approaches of the past, when "the scene was set" and one followed "the script." Contemporary poetry must deal with commonplace realities and not with the stock themes ("souvenirs") of classical and romantic poetry. The fictive nature of poetry is expressed through the theatrical metaphor.

"Of Mere Being" (p. 583)

The "palm at the end of the mind" is not a figure for some figment of reason, an image concealing an idea, except to the extent that it suggests all those things that are not ideas but simply and utterly *things*. The "bronze distance" and "the gold-feathered bird" suggest artifice—Yeats's "hammered gold" bird should come to mind here—a changeless thing with no relationship to what is human. Note the simple, objective sentences of the concluding lines which help to underscore the sense of distance from that which is living and changeable.

WILLIAM CARLOS WILLIAMS

(Note: Williams's "The Red Wheelbarrow" is discussed on pp. 433–34 in the "Elements of Poetry" section.)

"The Widow's Lament in Springtime" (p. 584)

The poem opens with a description of the speaker's change in perception suggesting a different relationship between the speaker and nature. This change is developed further in the poem. Discussion might center on the development of the opening metaphor.

"Spring and All" (p. 585)
This is another spring poem, but the setting and the mood are quite different. What is the effect of the setting? Why use a wasteland field near a "contagious hospital"? Is the parallel with human birth in the last three stanzas justified?

"Nantucket" (pp. 585–86)
This poem is composed of images which evoke a particular place. I have had some bizarre responses to the poem from students who did not know that Nantucket is a lovely island off the New England coast, and who did not carefully consider the connotations of the images in the poem. Asking students to insert a two-line image into the poem is one of the best ways I know to teach connotation. Or you can ask them to create a poem of their own about a special place using the same imagistic technique that Williams uses in this poem.

"This Is Just to Say" (p. 586)
"This is a poem?" is a fairly common response from students. Here is a good opportunity to examine the look of the poem. Why has the poet broken sentences as he has, why this particular arrangement of lines on the page? You can ask students to compose their own "I have eaten" poems to give them an idea of how important precision of word choice is to poetry. Or if you want to emphasize the importance of the line in poetry, bring in some want ads from a newspaper and have students construct found poems of them. (The personal ads in *The New York Review of Books* are big favorites with my students.)

"Flowers by the Sea" (p. 586)
Note the process here of the mind ordering and transforming its perception of flowers and sea so that one takes on the other's qualities.

"The Yachts" (p. 587)
Walter Sutton describes the poem's movement as one from "imagistic charm to symbolic horror" (*American Free Verse*). This poem may be discussed in Darwinian terms of survival of the fittest, and it has also been discussed in social terms, for it was written in the midst of the Depression (1935). Best to start, though, with close consideration of the imagery. How are humans described in the poem? How are the yachts described in the poem?
Compare: Bill Knott, "Survival of the Fittest Groceries" (pp. 448–49)

"The Last Words of My English Grandmother" (pp. 588–89)
You might want to ask students what their expectations were when they read the title of the poem. Did they expect something sentimental? Does

the speaker in the poem describe any of his feelings, or is he an objective observer?

Compare: Rosmarie Waldrop, "Stroke" (pp. 666–67)

"Landscape with the Fall of Icarus" (p. 589)

It is helpful to bring in a copy of Brueghel's painting when teaching this poem. At first reading, the poem may seem merely descriptive. You should point out the evaluative language: "the sea concerned with itself," "unsignificantly," "quite unnoticed," for example. Williams's interpretive and descriptive emphases should be compared with Auden's in "Musée des Beaux Arts."

MARIANNE MOORE

"Poetry" (pp. 590–91)

Your students' reactions to the opening words of the poem should be interesting. Of course, the poem goes on to describe the kind of poetry the speaker really dislikes: over-intellectualized, incomprehensible modern poetry ("we/ do not admire what/ we cannot understand"). Genuine poems are defined as "imaginary gardens with real toads in them," and poets are defined as "literalists of/ the imagination." Why is genuine poetry called "useful"? Do Moore's poems illustrate her definitions of poetry and the poet?

"The Fish" (pp. 591–92)

Moore is one of the closest and most precise observers of life. This poem presents lovely images in formal patterns. Note the unusual rhyme scheme, in which articles are sometimes used as rhyme words: "an/ injured fan," "the/ turquoise sea." The power of the sea is awesomely presented in the images of its action on the "defiant" rock.

Compare: Walt Whitman, "The World below the Brine" (pp. 540–41)
Robert Lowell, "Water" (pp. 628–29)

"A Jellyfish" (pp. 592–93)

Like "The Fish," this poem is an example of Moore's concept of "organic form." Just as the form of "The Fish" suggests change and flux and the movement of waves, so the structure of "A Jellyfish" imitates the opening and closing of this sea creature.

Compare: Emily Dickinson, "A Narrow Fellow in the Grass" (pp. 547–48)

"Nevertheless" (pp. 593–94)

The original title of this poem was "It Is Late, I Can Wait." You might ask students whether "Nevertheless" (which is also the first word of the poem) is a better title. The idea for the poem came to Moore when she found a flattened green strawberry at the bottom of a box of ripe red ones, and said, "Here's a strawberry that's had quite a struggle." (Quoted by Marguerite Young in "An Afternoon with Marianne Moore.") How do the images in the poem illustrate its theme: the inner strength that enables survival and success?

T. S. ELIOT

"The Love Song of J. Alfred Prufrock" (pp. 595–99)
If you wish to dig into all the allusions in Eliot's poetry, there are plenty of books and articles available. One of the most useful guides to Eliot's sources is Grover Smith, *T. S. Eliot's Poetry and Plays*. However, for students reading Eliot for the first time, the burden of Eliot's literary past may be quite overwhelming. I would suggest letting them discover Eliot through the patterns of imagery in the poetry, and the voices of the speakers. In the first 14 lines of "Prufrock," for example, we find the evening described as "Like a patient etherized upon a table," we are provoked with that "overwhelming question," and we meet the women who talk of Michelangelo. Following the threads of any or all of these should help students make connections in the poem. Why is the poem called a "Love Song"? How does the epigraph from Dante's *Inferno* influence the reading of the poem? How is this dramatic monologue similar to or different from Tennyson's "Ulysses"? If your students have read Marvell's "To His Coy Mistress," you might ask them what effect Eliot wished to create by referring to Marvell's poem in lines 92–93 of "Prufrock."

"Morning at the Window" (p. 599)
Considering the imagery here and its dehumanizing effect—disembodied souls, faces, that "aimless smile"—might be a good introduction to the longer poems.

"The Hollow Men" (pp. 599–602)
You might teach this poem as a further extension or attenuation of the state described in "Prufrock." The paradoxes of lines 11–12 recall Prufrock's inability to act taken a step further: actions are meaningless here. Again, a consideration of the imagery and its fragmented form is the best way into the poem. If your students have seen the film *Apocalypse Now* they may recall Marlon Brando's mumblings from this poem and be able to connect that portrayal of the senselessness of the Vietnam War with the spiritual emptiness of the post-World War I period described in "The Hollow Men." You might even start with the last section of the poem and the fragment of the Lord's Prayer ("For thine is the kingdom"). What is the rest of the prayer? Why can it not be completed?

"Journey of the Magi" (pp. 602–3)
The opening lines are adapted from a sermon preached by Lancelot Andrewes on Christmas day, 1622. The speaker is one of the magi, describing

his trip to Bethlehem. He is old now, and awaiting his own death; Christ's crucifixion has not yet occurred, so that this magus knows nothing about Atonement. What has happened to the speaker since his journey? How was his perception changed by the birth he witnessed? What is his attitude toward the birth of Christ?

Note, line 41: the old dispensation refers to the time before the birth of Christ.

"Macavity: The Mystery Cat" (pp. 603–4)
This poem appeared in *Old Possum's Book of Practical Cats* (1939), and provides an example of the whimsical Eliot, whose favorite animal was, of course, the cat. It's fun to work with the metrics of this poem. How would you describe the speaker of this poem and his relationship with Macavity?

E. E. CUMMINGS

"Buffalo Bill's" (pp. 604–5)
This poem can serve to introduce students to Cummings's innovations in typography—the visual perception of language—his flouting of grammatical rules, his rhetorical use of punctuation, and his use of colloquial American diction. Consider the attitude of the speaker in this poem. Is this poem a tribute to Buffalo Bill?

"Spring is like a perhaps hand" (p. 605)
Who else would personify Spring as a window dresser? What is the effect of the use of parentheses in the poem?
    Compare: William Carlos Williams, "Spring and All" (p. 585)

"next to of course god america i" (pp. 605–6)
This is a nice example of Fourth-of-July political rhetoric. The poem has 14 lines. Is it a sonnet? There are two speakers in the poem. What is the effect of the last speaker's comment?

"somewhere i have never travelled" (p. 606)
Note the opening and closing rhythms in this poem, moving toward and away from "the heart of this flower" in the heart of the poem, and the use of the rose metaphor.

"r-p-o-p-h-e-s-s-a-g-r" (pp. 606–7)
Here's another place for a discussion of how a poem looks on the page. You might ask students to try their own insect, fish, or animal poems using this one as a model.

"my father moved through dooms of love" (pp. 607–9)
Discussion might start with the use of paradox that runs throughout the poem ("haves of give," "depths of height") developing a sense of the

all-encompassing, unifying world of the father. The use of simile should be discussed as well. Which ones contribute most? Which least?

Compare: Theodore Roethke, "My Papa's Waltz" (pp. 618–619)

"pity this busy monster" (p. 609)
The tension in this poem is expressed by "A world of made/ is not a world of born." What is the attitude toward mankind expressed by "We doctors"?

"Who's Who" (p. 610)
Here is a nice example of the function of the octet-sestet division of a sonnet. The octet deals with "the facts," the actions which entitle one to be included in *Who's Who,* and the sestet describes one who lives the contemplative life. What does the poem tell us about the relationship of these two people?

"On This Island" (pp. 610–11)
As a nature poem, this poem might be compared with Wordsworth's "I Wandered Lonely as a Cloud," in its emphasis on perception of nature, the entrance of nature into self, and the importance of memory.

"As I Walked Out One Evening" (pp. 611–13)
Auden uses some of the strategies and themes that we find in Marvell's "To His Coy Mistress": hyperbole, the passage of time and its personification, the persuasion to love. But can we consider Auden's a *carpe diem* poem? Stephen Spender has said that "Essentially the direction of Auden's poetry has been toward defining the concept of love." How is love defined here? To what effect are images of fertility and infertility used in the poem?

"Lullaby" (pp. 613–14)
What connotations does the title of the poem have? How does the poem deviate from a conventional lullaby? What forces in the poem might be considered as in opposition to human love? How would you define the human love described in this poem?

"Musée des Beaux Arts" (p. 614)
This poem can be taught with Williams's "The Fall of Icarus" (p. 589), and you might consider pairing it with Eliot's "Journey of the Magi" (pp. 602–3). Both poems stress human ordinariness and its reaction to an extraordinary event.

"In Memory of W. B. Yeats" (pp. 615–16)
How does this poem compare with other elegies in the text? To what extent is the poem about Yeats? About the speaker? About poetry? What is the effect of the change of rhythm in the last section of the poem?

Compare: Marianne Moore, "Poetry" (pp. 590–91)

"The Unknown Citizen" (p. 617)

How would you describe the speaker in this poem? What is this citizen being praised for? What social comment is being made here? Or, a related question would be, how is each one of us interpreted by our society? Students can write their own "unknown citizen" poems; no names, of course, just social security numbers.

"The Premonition" (p. 618)

The image of "Hair on a narrow wrist bone" leaps out of this poem much as Donne's "bracelet of bright hair about the bone" leaps out of "The Relic." How does Roethke's image evoke a feeling of mortality in this poem? "The Premonition" may be compared with Hopkins's "Spring and Fall" (p. 550), or with other "father" poems, such as Roethke's "My Papa's Waltz" (pp. 618–19), Cummings's "my father moved through dooms of love" (pp. 607–9) an Plath's "Daddy" (pp. 658–60).

"My Papa's Waltz" (pp. 618–19)

The physical sensations experienced by the boy should be discussed. Were these sensations pleasant or unpleasant? What does the description of the mother contribute to the poem? The poem is addressed to the father. Would the poem be interpreted differently if the third person were used instead?

"Old Florist" (p. 619)

This poem looks like a little catalogue of actions performed by this old florist. Attention should be paid to the denotations and connotations of these actions and the portrait they provide of this man.

"Dolor" (p. 619)

The title of the poem describes the mood of the poem, and the mood is defined through an extended metaphor. There is an interesting mixture of abstract and concrete language in the poem which will repay discussion. Would the poem be any different if there were no "I" present?

Compare: W. H. Auden, "The Unknown Citizen" (p. 617)

"Elegy for Jane" (p. 619–20)

Natural imagery abounds in this poem, forming a portrait of Jane—or, we might say, of Jane as she is perceived by the speaker. The last five lines of the poem almost always provoke a discussion of the relationship between the speaker and Jane (yes, Jane was Roethke's student, but he knew her only slightly).

Compare: see p. 60 in this manual for suggested elegies for comparison.

"The Waking" (pp. 620–21)

This poem resists any attempt at close paraphrasing. It might be approached as a relative of the *carpe diem* poem, with "I wake to sleep" translated as "I am born to die." There is a celebration of sense experience ("We think by feeling") and an admonition to seize the day ("so take the lively air"). If your students are interested in form, compare this poem with Dylan Thomas's "Do Not Go Gentle into That Good Night," which is also a villanelle. The villanelle is a risky form to use because of the amount of rhyme repetition, and you may want to discuss which poet was more successful in employing this form.

"I Knew a Woman" (p. 621)

Movement is one of the major themes in this love poem. "Turn, and Counter-turn, and Stand" are English terms for the structure of the Pindaric ode—strophe, antistrophe, epode—a structure which reflects the dance pattern used in classical Greek theater. The speaker's attitudes toward movement and time—time as pattern, time as eternity—should be discussed as well as the patterns of movement in the poem.

Compare: Robert Herrick, "Upon Julia's Clothes" (p. 492)

DYLAN THOMAS

Thomas is a very dramatic and mellifluous reader of his poetry, but if you plan to use his recordings in class, be sure you've discussed some of the poetry first. Students are frequently overwhelmed by the glorious sound and pay no attention to the sense.

"The Force That through the Green Fuse Drives the Flower" (pp. 622–23)

A microcosm-macrocosm parallel structures this poem, which expresses the feeling of being caught in and part of the cycle of nature. Why "green fuse" and not "green stem"? What is the effect of the repetition of "And I am dumb to tell"?

"This Bread I Break" (p. 623)

The bread and wine immediately suggest the Eucharist, and rightly so. However, the religious imagery here is extended into nature and art, as the last line suggests.

"A Refusal to Mourn the Death, by Fire, of a Child . . ." (pp. 623–24)

If students have read Housman's "To an Athlete Dying Young," they should have some idea of the elegiac conventions Thomas refuses to use in this poem. Why are old conventions such as "it is good to die young" inappropriate? Here you might mention that the poem was written after a bombing raid on London during World War II. As in the previous poem, there is religious imagery throughout, but it is secularized, as in lines 7–12. The "first death" refers not only to Christ, but also to the child, "London's daughter."

Compare: see p. 60 in this manual for suggested elegies for comparison.

"Do Not Go Gentle into That Good Night" (p. 624)

The specific subject of this poem is Thomas's father, who was dying of cancer. You can approach this poem from an opposite point of view: what does it mean to "go gentle" into death?

Compare: John Donne, "Death be not proud" (p. 489)

"Fern Hill" (pp. 625–26)

Fern Hill was a farm belonging to Ann Jones, Thomas's aunt, and Thomas spent many youthful holidays there. Here again, the theme of being caught in time is present. This reflective poem evokes the feeling of how it was to be young, when life did seem to go on in a timeless state ("And once below a time"). Discussion might center on the double vision of the speaker, juxtaposing his carefree younger self in an Edenic landscape with an older, presumably wiser and sadder self who knows that the farm of his youth can no longer exist for him ("the farm forever fled from the childless land").

Compare: Gerard Manley Hopkins, "Spring and Fall" (p. 550)

ROBERT LOWELL

"To Speak of Woe That Is in Marriage" (p. 627)

The title of this poem comes from the opening of the Prologue of Chaucer's "Wife of Bath's Tale":

> Experience, though noon auctoritee
> Were in this world, is right ynogh for me
> To speke of wo that is in marriage

The Wife of Bath definitely is qualified to speak from experience: she's had five husbands.

The use of quotation marks in title, epigraph, and poem emphasize the three "experienced" speakers: the Wife of Bath, the German philosopher Schopenhauer, and the wife who speaks in the poem. This poem can serve as an entrance into the other Lowell poems in the anthology. In Lowell's poems there is an identifiable speaker presenting a particular psychological landscape. Attention to the images in the poems will help to define these landscapes and the stance of each speaker. (For a study of Lowell's images, see Marjorie Perloff, *The Poetic Art of Robert Lowell*.)

"Skunk Hour" (pp. 627–28)

In Lowell's words, the opening of the poem gives "a dawdling more or less amiable picture of a declining Maine sea town." The speaker is also in a decline, or dark night of the soul, as the adaptation of Lucifer's line in *Paradise Lost* makes clear: "which way I fly is Hell; myself am Hell" (IV:75). The skunks are the strongest life force in this dismal landscape, and discussion might center on description of their actions as opposed to the actions—or lack of them—of the humans here.

Notes: Line 15: L.L. Bean's is a Maine mail order house which specializes in hunting and fishing clothes. These clothes are considered fashionable by those who neither hunt nor fish. Line 18: red fox stain. "Meant to describe the rusty reddish color of autumn on Blue Hill, a Maine mountain near where we were living" (Lowell's note). Line 32: "Careless Love" was a popular song in the late fifties.

"Water" (pp. 628–29)

In this reflective poem, time present and its mood alternate with the mood of time past. What connotations are associated with the word "rock" (which is repeated throughout the poem)? Why is the poem entitled "Water"? What does the dream image in stanza 7 suggest about the relationship of the man and the woman?

"For the Union Dead" (pp. 629–31)

The relationship of the past (Civil War) to the present (civil rights) and the changes that have and are taking place structure the poem. The speaker's past and present are part of the structure as well. The patterns of imagery in the poem should be closely examined. For example, those connected with the Aquarium, such as fish, bubbles. balloons, and those connected with the reptilian underworld come together in the last lines of the poem in those "giant finned cars." (You may have to explain to students that fifties cars were enormous and did indeed have fins.) What sort of a hero was Colonel Shaw? Why is "compass-needle" used as a simile to describe him?

Notes: In his epigraph, Lowell has altered slightly the Latin motto of the Society of the Cincinnati which is on the monument: *Omnia relinquit servare rempublicam* (He gives up everything to serve the republic). The change from singular to plural is of some significance to the poem. Line 28: William James, the philosopher and psychologist, delivered the oration when the monument was dedicated in 1897.

GWENDOLYN BROOKS

"The Mother" (pp. 632–33)

The tone of this poem and the different rhythms of its lines should be emphasized in discussion, if only to avoid having students seize on this powerful poem as an anti-abortion tract to the neglect of the craft that produces its exquisite sadness. Or you can plunge right in and ask whether "The Mother" is an ironic title.

Compare: Adrienne Rich, "Night-Pieces: For a Child" (pp. 650–51)

"Kitchenette Building" (p. 633)

Who—or what—is speaking here? "We are things of dry hours" is reminiscent of Eliot's "We are the hollow men," and a similar kind of dehumanization would seem to be suggested here. Unlike Eliot's poem, however, there is a sense of life in this kitchenette building. How would you describe its inhabitants? This poem works well with Baraka's "Ka 'Ba," which treats a similar situation, but urges a different voice for the "things" of kitchenette buildings.

"The Rites for Cousin Vit" (pp. 633–34)

In this poem and in "We Real Cool," diction and rhythm are of considerable importance. And you might ask how this poem works as a sonnet.

Compare: E. E. Cummings, "Buffalo Bill's" (pp. 604–5)

"We Real Cool" (p. 634)

You might write the poem on the blackboard in complete sentences:

> We real cool.
> We left school. Etc.

Have students read this version and then the original aloud to hear the difference in rhythm—how the original version's jazzy beat is lost with end-stopped lines.

"The Lovers of the Poor" (pp. 634–36)

How does the use of alliteration contribute to the tone of this poem? Alliteration forces us to read more slowly and to focus on sequences of words. Brooks wishes to create different effects: the liquid sarcasm of "Their League is allotting largesse to the Lost" contrasts sharply with the description of the kitten in the previous line, "hunched-up, haggard, to-be-hurt," and serves to emphasize the difference between the world of the Ladies and the world of the Poor.

W. S. MERWIN

"Separation" (p. 637)

This is a good poem with which to begin a poetry course. Good poetry violates our expectations, and this poem is an excellent example of that. "Your absence has gone through me" sets up the expectation of something sharp, like a knife, being used as a simile. Although there is a needle here, it is the *thread* that provides the simile. And what is the color of absence? As Robert Scholes has pointed out, "Merwin is a poet of absence and presence, departure and—less frequently—return." Such poetry resists a mimetic type of interpretation—and it's meant to. Working with the images and the mood they evoke is a useful way to proceed. "Separation" may be compared with "When You Go Away," which presents a series of images evoking emptiness and loneliness. You can ask students to free-associate, or freewrite for ten minutes on the word "absence." Out of this they might well create their own poems, using "Separation" or "When You Go Away" as models.

"Things" (p. 637)
Note the poem's two-part structure and ask what kinds of rhetorical strategies the things make upon the possessor. Why are the things addressing the gentleman in this manner? What is *he* feeling? Is the persuasion an effective one? You might ask students to talk about their own possessions: what sort of grip do objects (from keepsakes to stereos) have on them?

"Economy" (p. 638)
It will be helpful to catalogue the ways in which the poem manipulates the proverb. Why do mirrors usually break? Why would anyone want to break a mirror? What's the difference between seven years of bad luck and seven years of sorrow? What does a shattered mirror look like? What does it mean to have a shattered face? What is behind such a face? Who is holding it up? Is it economical?

"Departure's Girl-Friend" (pp. 638–39)
The first time I taught this poem, I simply said to my students, "I'm not at all sure what it means." I'm still not sure. However, here's an attempt at a paraphrase. The poem describes a thwarted attempt to redefine departure (the absence that causes loneliness for someone) into a positive, celebrated event (the wreath "my boat"). The stone wharf is the pure undecorated reality: to depart is to be absent. Thus, our imaginary fortifications are demolished. We're thrown back into the "hated city" of flux and change and the immediacy of now, of chance, of instability. Our only defense against this life is a "Buoy of flowers," which might represent the fictions we invent and live in order to endure in a world of constant change.

"When You Go Away" (p. 639)
This poem is a series of images, and their connotations should be worked through carefully. What changes are described in the first 5 lines? What does the speaker go through at night? What value does he place on his words? Is the last simile appropriate?

"Tale" (p. 639)
Account for the title of this poem.

"Elegy" (p. 639)

This poem should be compared with Dylan Thomas's "A Refusal to Mourn . . . ," for this is a refusal to elegize, and its meaning depends on the reader knowing the conventions of the elegy.

"The Morning" (p. 640)

Why is the speaker surprised? Where is the couple? What are the connotations of the season, and the petals and leaves? How are the petals and leaves related to the lover's body? You will also want to note the rhyme of lines 4 and 9, and ask students how lines 8 and 9 are related. Consider, too, the use of synesthesia as a metaphor for union.

PHILIP LEVINE

"For Fran" (pp. 640–41)

The opening stanza connects Fran with the life force in its battle against death (winter). How is this theme developed in the poem?

"Hold Me" (pp. 641–42)

This poem, like so many of Levine's, uses the things of everyday life to create strong, startling images. How is a person defined? How are we known? What if we are not seen by others? These are some of the questions raised here. A way into this poem is to ask how the poem explains— perhaps even provokes—its title.

"No One Remembers" (pp. 642–44)

This poem can be compared with "Hold Me." It might well be presented as a poem which contradicts its title, for Uncle Joe is remembered by at least one person. Like "Ricky" it is a kind of elegy, and the relationship of speaker and subject is a main issue. As a writing exercise, you might ask students to produce a short life history of Uncle Joe, perhaps in the form of an obituary.

"Ricky" (pp. 644–48)

There is much about this elegy that might be compared and contrasted with Milton's "Lycidas," especially in its use of nature. Ricky's drowning, the speaker's fear of water, the relentless sun, the rage it seems to inspire both recall the conventions of the pastoral elegy and at the same time we are aware that such conventions are being transformed by a twentieth-century sensibility. For here, nature acts on man, and does not merely mirror his moods.

Compare: other suggested elegies for comparison may be found on p. 60.

"Let Me Begin Again" (p. 648)

If at this point in the semester you are less than pleased with your students' responses to poetry, see Ellen Strenski and Nancy Giller Esposito, "The Poet, the Computer, and the Classroom" in *College English* 42 (October, 1980) 142–150. "Let Me Begin Again" and another of Levine's poems were pitted against a poem by a computer. Levine won, but the reasons why will chill you.

The last two lines of this poem might well be the starting place for discussion of individuality or of "if I entered my life knowing what I know now" types of writing.

ADRIENNE RICH

"The Afterwake" (p. 649)

Who is the "you" in this poem? What is the relationship between the speaker and this other person? How does the midwife analogy help to explain this relationship?

"Novella" (pp. 649–50)

The title should be discussed. How does it relate to the form of this poem?

"Night-Pieces: For a Child" (pp. 650–51)

Some students may have difficulty with this poem because of the "mother" theme: how the child perceives the mother, how the mother perceives her relationship with the child. You may want to concentrate on the two dreams and how dreams affect our waking vision. Or consider the structure of the poem: why is it so clearly divided into two sections?

  Compare: Philip Levine, "No One Remembers"
       Sylvia Plath, "Edge"

"5:30 A.M." (p. 651)

Why the comparison with the fox? "Miracles escapes" from what? Pregnancy, perhaps, dependence on pills. Who is the killer here?

"Moving in Winter" (pp. 651–52)

You might compare this poem with Merwin's "Things," though here the emphasis is on the connotations of our possessions, how they reveal themselves against a different landscape. How do the memories connected with the pieces of furniture define a particular relationship?

"Rape" (pp. 652–53)

The incongruity in the first line "both prowler and father" should provide a way into the poem, for the poem describes a situation in which the familiar becomes suddenly and awfully strange. Imagery should be carefully noted: much of it is connected with "machinery," which has distinctly masculine and oppressive connotations in this poem. Also, what is the effect of the repetition and the rhythm it creates?

Compare: Sylvia Plath, "Daddy" (pp. 658–60)

"Amnesia" (p. 653)
There is direct reference in this poem to the film *Citizen Kane,* and if you are using *Elements 5,* you should refer to the film section, and ideally, screen the film for your students. The poem can also be taught effectively without reference to the film because it does refer to a more general situation: that of becoming a man in American culture. What is that "something that gets left behind"?

GARY SNYDER

"Mid-August at Sourdough Mountain Lookout" (p. 654)
A specific mood is developed here through the contrast between what is down in the valley and what it is like high on the mountain. The speaker's relationship with nature, and the oppositions of heat and cold, below and above, should be explored.

"Riprap" (pp. 654–55)
This is a statement about poetry, the creation of which is compared with the creation of rock. There is also the comparison of words and rocks, and typographically, the poem on the page may be said to resemble riprap. The notion of change, the endless game of Go (which is played with black and white stones), should be carefully noted. In no way is the poem a rock, or monument, for riprap, though it reinforces and strengthens, is a relatively loose arrangement. Snyder describes riprap as "a cobble of stone laid on steep slick rock to make a trail for horses in the mountain." He describes poetry as "a riprap on the slick rock of metaphysics."

"An Autumn Morning at Shokoku-ji" (p. 655)
The stars watched by the speaker are of some importance to the poem. The Pleiades are a loose cluster of stars in the constellation Taurus, named after the seven daughters of Atlas, who were transformed into stars. Jupiter, the supreme god of the Romans, rules law and weather. Venus, the goddess of love, was "Mother of Earth and Heaven" to her Roman worshippers. Of interest to this poem is Jane Harrison's description of Aphrodite, Venus's Greek counterpart: "She is never wife, never tolerates permanent patriarchal wedlock . . . her will is for love, not marriage" (*A Prolegomena to the Study of Greek Religion*).

"It Was When" (pp. 656)
This is a celebration of love in a family situation, ending with "the grace" of conception. Some students might notice that the woman is presented in

several synechdoches; the question is, do the parts add up to a whole woman? You might pursue the effect produced by the descriptions of bodies moving in nature.

"Sheep in Fog" (pp. 657–58)

The speaker's perception of nature and how she sees herself perceived by "People or stars" is of interest here. Through the speaker's eyes, nature transforms itself: "hills step off into whiteness," "morning has been blackening," fields "threaten." Does the poem explain why "I disappoint them"?

"Daddy" (pp. 658–60)

The insistent rhythm and the repetitions in the rhyme scheme should certainly be discussed, but obviously the images and the autobiographical content will be of immediate interest. And it is an interest that Plath herself provoked when at a reading, she provided this introduction to the poem:

> The poem is spoken by a girl with an Electra complex. Her father died while she thought he was God. Her case is complicated by the fact that her father was also a Nazi and her mother was very possibly part Jewish. In the daughter the two strains marry and paralyze each other—she has to act out the awful little allegory before she is free of it. (A. Alvarez in Charles Newmann, ed., *The Art of Sylvia Plath*.)

One way to open discussion is to offer up Alvarez's opinion: "Despite everything, 'Daddy' is a love poem." It's likely that you'll have to explain some of those Nazi references to your students. They will not know that the Luftwaffe was the German air force, or that a "panzer-man" drives a tank (and the Nazi panzer divisions were extremely powerful), or that Adolf Hitler wrote *Mein Kampf* (My Life).

"Kindness" (pp. 660–61)

The tone here may puzzle your students. It is, of course, ironic—until the last three lines. The sugared personification of kindness is contrasted with the reality of "the cry of a child." And why is the child's cry compared with a rabbit's? Disturbing also is the image of those "Japanese silks . . . anaesthetized." What relation does the "you" in line 16 have with Dame Kindness?

"Edge" (p. 661)

One of Plath's last poems, this one is very imagistic, suggesting a marble grave monument, or a painting on a classical Greek urn. Many Greek vase paintings feature a mother-goddess characterized by twin babies; often she represents Night with Sleep and Death. "The woman is perfected" suggests both the perfection of death and the perfection of motherhood. The speaker's attitude toward the later should provide subject matter for discussion.

"Words" (p. 662)

This is a poem about poetry, and its pattern of imagery is notable for a chain of transformations: axe-echoes-horses; sap-tears-water-mirror; rock-skull. Note in the final transformation, words-hoof-taps, a change from metaphor to metonymy. Note also the end of movement: the mirror has been reestablished as "the pool."

IMAMU AMIRI BARAKA (LEROI JONES)

"The Turncoat" (pp. 662–63)

This is an early poem, romantic and "literary." Certainly its Keatsian consciousness of a double self calls up the Clark Kent-Superman transformation. How does the sea function in this poem? What is the speaker's attitude toward fantasy?

"Ka 'Ba" (p. 663)

Here is a more militant Baraka, urging his people to celebrate their African heritage, and to be reborn out of it.

Compare: William Blake, "London" (p. 502)

"Legacy" (pp. 663–64)

This is a poem that moves, pushed along by a piling up of gerunds and gerund phrases toward the "pretend sea." What does the sea symbolize in this poem? Why is the poem dedicated to "Blues People"?

"An Agony. As Now." (pp. 664–65)

Like "The Turncoat," this poem is about a dual self, here quite clearly the body and the soul. The images connected with each should be traced carefully.

Compare: John Donne, "I am a little world made cunningly" (pp. 488–89)
Robert Lowell, "Skunk Hour" (pp. 627–28)
Sylvia Plath, "Daddy" (pp. 658–60)

ROSMARIE WALDROP

"Deflecting Forces" (p. 666)

You might start by asking what the terrifying visions of the third-to-last line might be. What is terrifying about a hurricane? How does the image of the hurricane as an unreasoning, chaotic, natural force widen into an image of the whole natural order? Your students should know that a scream is a deflected force. Some students may note that PROVIDENCE HURRICANE BARRIER (a movable seawall designed to protect the city from inundation) marks a formal division between two parts of the poem. They may want to develop a contrast between the solidity of both imagery and line in the first part of the poem to the instability of both in the second part ("rest/ is a particular kind/ of movement/ on the moving earth/ our element's unstable"). As a final challenge, ask your students to grapple with the ambiguity of the title: is "forces" the subject or object of "deflecting"?

"Stroke" (pp. 666–67)

Why does the poem end as it does? In what ways is the sudden silence or disconnection appropriate to the subject and language of the poem? You may want to point out that "won't" is the last word of the first and final lines, and ask students to look for other such symmetries and connections. The poem begins and ends with extremities. We begin without a leg to stand on. We end by losing hold.

From "The Road is Everywhere or Stop This Body"

Waldrop has written about this sequence, "Sitting in the car is the basic situation. I have negative feelings about this: the increased isolation as I put this extra metal shell between me and the environment and, of course, the statistical likelihood that the car will become my coffin. But there is also the pleasure and excitement of speed which I try to get at by having one sentence tumble into the next, as it were. (The object of one sentence turns into the subject of the next without being repeated: The body's angle . . . surrenders its shadow. Its shadow falls back behind the metal's pull. The metal's pull . . .) The book as a whole cuts from traffic to other circulation systems: breath, blood, sex, money, language, and to the seasons. . . ."

Students are likely to have problems with the syntactical complexities of this poetry, and it is probably best to begin with several oral readings of each section. You may want to point out that any route through these poems is likely to be problematic, both frustrating and deeply rewarding, and that the reader is likely to enjoy the poems to the extent that he or she feels comfortable in the driver's seat. This can be a very good place to talk about the art of reading, about the *various* kinds of pleasure any text has to offer. Ask your students to compare the reader's expectations and the demands the poet puts upon the reader in section 78 to those of Shakespeare's sonnet 130. In what ways are the open-endedness and difficulty of Waldrop's poetry as appropriate to our day as the use of Elizabethan conventions were in Shakespeare's? How does Waldrop's use of traffic signs (especially in 78) compare with Shakespeare's use of eyes, hair, teeth and the like in his parody of the Petrarchan poem? How does Waldrop's vision of the human body compare with Shakespeare's?

ACKNOWLEDGMENT: I wish to thank my colleague, John Martone, for his excellent suggestions and his help in the writing of the poetry section of this manual. The suggestions for teaching Rosmarie Waldrop's poetry are entirely his, and some of the approaches to Shakespeare, Donne, and Merwin are his also.

N.R.C.

Drama

CARL H. KLAUS

DESIGN, SCOPE, AND FLEXIBILITY OF THE DRAMA SECTION

In the Drama section of our anthology (pp. 673–1263), you and your students will find a critical introduction to drama (pp. 673–700), and a collection of twelve plays (pp. 701–1263). Our critical section provides discussions of both the theatrical and the literary contexts of drama (pp. 673–84), of the modes of drama—tragedy, comedy, satire, romance, and tragicomedy (pp. 685–94), and of the elements of drama—dialogue, plot, and character (pp. 695–700). Each section explains concepts that are basic to the understanding of drama and shows how those concepts can be used to analyze representative plays such as those included in the collection. As an additional aid to studying plays and writing about them, we have provided a Glossary of Critical Terms at the end of the book.

The collection contains outstanding plays by major dramatists from the Classical period to the contemporary period. These plays exemplify the basic contexts, modes, and elements of drama that are discussed in the critical section. We have arranged the plays chronologically, since that order provides the handiest system for locating selections. For the same reason, we have divided the collection into two parts: Classical to Neoclassical Drama, and Modern to Contemporary Drama. As a special aid to understanding the theatrical context of plays in the first part, we have included prefatory notes about the theaters in which they were originally produced (the notes for the Classical, Renaissance, and Neoclassical plays also contain line drawings to illustrate the basic components of each theater). As an aid to understanding the theatrical context of plays in the second part, we have included a prefatory note on setting and symbolism in modern and contemporary drama.

The seven modern plays in the second part of our collection, together with the five traditional plays in the first part, provide far more material, we realize, than you will be able to use in your course. But in this, as in other sections of our anthology, we have aimed to produce a collection which is flexible enough to meet the varying needs of many instructors and students. And flexibility can only be achieved by giving too much rather than not enough. The size of our collection, together with the design of our critical section, will enable you to choose among a variety of approaches and corresponding plays, rather than having a single approach and restricted set of plays imposed upon you. You will have enough plays to assign for class discussion, independent reading, and paper assignments. And your students will still be left with plays to read for their own interest and pleasure.

Given the flexibility of our drama section, your only problem will be to decide which approach to take in teaching the plays, and which plays will best suit your approach. To help you make those decisions is one of our main purposes here. Thus you will find in the pages that follow not only comments on each of the individual plays, but also an explanation of several different approaches you can take to drama, along with a discussion of the plays and the critical sections that will best suit each approach.

APPROACHES TO TEACHING DRAMA

The critical apparatus in our anthology is designed to facilitate a variety of approaches to drama. In fact, it sets forth all the basic approaches that currently prevail in the teaching of drama. Thus we will use it as a guide for organizing this section, and we will discuss the approaches in the order in which they are taken up in the apparatus. The organization of our apparatus (and of this section) is not, of course, meant to be prescriptive. In fact, we have written the apparatus so that it can either be read straight through from beginning to end, or be studied part by part according to any order you wish. Though the separate parts are complementary, they do not depend upon one another for comprehension. Thus you can assign any part of the critical apparatus that suits your approach and be confident that your students can follow it without having to read the others.

Under each of the following categories, you will find a brief description of the approach, a guide to using the relevant part of the critical apparatus, and a discussion of appropriate plays. Choosing an approach is, of course, your business. Thus we will not recommend any one as being preferable to the others. Here, then, is a description of some approaches that you can choose from in the teaching of drama.

DRAMA AND THEATRICAL PERFORMANCE

This approach emphasizes the reading of plays as scripts for theatrical performance. If you take this approach you will be able to show students how to read a text so that they can either stage it accurately in their own minds, or appreciate an actual stage production of it. Though this approach necessarily focuses on the text as a set of cues for production, its aim is not to teach the discovery of spectacle as an end in itself, but to develop an awareness of spectacle as a means to understanding and enjoying drama. By approaching the text as a set of theatrical cues, you will be able to engage the imaginative interest of your students in drama and encourage them to read dialogue closely for its implications.

To introduce this approach you can have your students read the critical section on "Drama and Theatrical Performance" (pp. 674–79). This section provides a definition of theatrical spectacle, a discussion of the various elements that contribute to spectacle, and an explanation of how to analyze a text so as to discover and understand the particular spectacle that is implied by its dialogue. Our explanation includes a sample analysis of a passage from *Othello,* which first shows them how to infer such basic elements as blocking, movement, and gestures, and then shows them how to infer the total staging of the passage both in a modern theater and in its original Renaissance theater, the Globe. This section of the critical apparatus, together with the prefatory theatrical notes, can serve as a basic resource to guide your students in approaching drama theatrically.

In conjunction with the critical section, you would do well to have your students read the entire first act of *Othello,* so that they understand the full dramatic context of the passage we have analyzed. Then, as an immediate follow-up to this assignment, you might ask a group of students to volunteer to do a very simple in-class staging and reading of the sample *Othello* passage (working only with blocking, movement, and gestures). This activity will give them a chance both to experience the tangible results of a theatrical analysis and to check our analysis for its accuracy to the text and appropriateness to the purpose of the scene as a whole. Once your students have read, staged, and judged our sample analysis, you might then assign them another brief passage from the first act of *Othello,* either for class discussion, staging, or a written theatrical analysis.

By the time you have completed this introductory sequence of assignments, your students will have acquired some basic techniques for identifying theatrical cues and using them to visualize and understand the staging of a brief bit of dramatic interaction. Then they will be ready to move on to longer scenes and sequences of scenes—in the third and fourth acts of *Othello,* for example—taking into account not only such basic elements as blocking and movement, but also the more subtle aspects of performance, such as facial expression, intonation, posture, and pacing. To infer these aspects your students will have to analyze not only particular cues in the text but also important dramatic elements such as character, mood, situation, and plot. They will, in short, have to interpret the action in order to envision a performance of the action.

As a final discussion topic, or written project, on *Othello,* you might have your students consider alternative stagings of the bedchamber scene in the fifth act. Ask them, for example, to imagine a Renaissance as opposed to a modern staging of the scene. As preparation for this problem they should review our comparison of Renaissance and modern stagings (pp. 678–79), as well as our detailed description of the Renaissance stage (pp. 814–16).

By following this step-by-step schedule of activities for *Othello* (or any other traditional play in the collection), you will be able not only to cover the work as a whole, but also to give your students a systematic and purposeful introduction to all of the important elements of theater. You can then proceed to study the impact of different theaters and different modes of drama on theatrical performance. To facilitate such a study we suggest that you choose a group of four or five additional plays in the collection which are thematically related to *Othello*—plays dealing with the problems of love and jealousy, trust and betrayal, illusion and reality. By studying works that share these common themes, your class will have a natural basis on which to make distinctions between the theatrical effects of different stages and different modes of drama.

Here, then, is a list of appropriate plays together with suggested readings in the critical apparatus and prefatory theatrical notes.

The Misanthrope, pp. 914–64.
"Satire and Romance," pp. 690–92
"Satire on the Neoclassical Stage," pp. 912–13

A Doll's House, pp. 969–1028
"Tragicomedy, Naturalism, and Absurdist Drama," pp. 692–94
"Setting and Symbolism in Modern and Contemporary Drama," pp. 965–68

The Stronger, pp. 1029–33
"Tragicomedy, Naturalism, and Absurdist Drama," pp. 692–94
"Setting and Symbolism in Modern and Contemporary Drama," pp. 965–68

The Threepenny Opera, pp.1104–65
"Satire and Romance," pp. 690–92
"Setting and Symbolism in Modern and Contemporary Drama," pp. 965–68

Mother and Child, pp. 1166–72
"Tragicomedy, Naturalism, and Absurdist Drama," pp. 692–94
"Setting and Symbolism in Modern and Contemporary Drama," pp. 965–68

Cat on a Hot Tin Roof, pp. 1173–1255
"Tragicomedy, Naturalism, and Absurdist Drama," pp. 692–94
"Setting and Symbolism in Modern and Contemporary Drama," pp. 965–68

As a special supplement to this theatrical approach, you might also consider showing your students film productions which are available for three of the plays in our collection: *Othello*, starring Laurence Olivier; *A Doll's House*, starring Claire Bloom; and *Cat on a Hot Tin Roof*, starring Burl Ives and Elizabeth Taylor. Before showing any of these films you might direct your students to focus on a single scene, or sequence of scenes, and have them compare the film production with their own theatrical interpretation of the text.

As a concluding class project for this approach, you might invite several pairs of students to stage a series of in-class performances of *The Stronger*. It is an extremely short play, running to only three and one-half pages in our text, requiring only a couple of performers, a couple of tables, a few chairs, and a few props. Thus it will give students the opportunity to prepare and witness varying theatrical interpretations of an entire play.

DRAMA AND OTHER LITERARY FORMS

This approach uses the other literary forms—fiction, poetry, and the essay—to help students develop an understanding of drama. Thus it is a particularly appropriate method to use if, like many other instructors, you organize your course to take up drama after the other literary forms—and before film. This approach assumes, of course, that the four forms of literature do not exist in airtight compartments, but rather that each form is capable of drawing upon elements, techniques, and strategies of the others. This view of the literary forms and their interdependence is presented in the general introduction to our anthology, "The Forms of Literature" (pp. xxiii–xxvii), and it is elaborated in the critical section, "Drama and Other Literary Forms" (pp. 679–80). Thus you can prepare students for this approach by having them read and discuss this material before beginning a study of the plays themselves. In this way your students will also be reviewing the forms they have already studied and applying what they have learned to an even more complex form of literature.

Once you have established for your students the critical framework appropriate to this approach, you can then examine individual plays in relation to the literary forms with which they are most closely allied, or on which they most heavily depend for their effect. To facilitate this study you can follow the organization of our critical section, "Drama and Other Literary Forms," which first takes up "Drama and Narration" (pp. 680–82), then "Drama and Meditation" (pp. 682–83), and finally "Drama and Persuasion" (p. 684). Thus you can first study plays that depend heavily on fictional, or narrative, techniques; then plays that rely heavily on poetic, or meditative, techniques; and finally plays that use the persuasive strategies of the essay.

If you choose a different pair of plays to study in connection with each of the literary forms, you will then be able to cover a total of six plays in all—an ample number for an introductory study of drama. Further, if in each pairing you include one play from the "Classical to Neoclassical" collection and one play from the "Modern to Contemporary" collection, you will be able to compare traditional and modern techniques in each case, and you will be assured of introducing your students to a broadly historical range of drama.

Here, then, is a classification of the plays appropriate for study in relation to each of the literary forms, along with brief notes about pertinent elements that you might focus on each work.

Drama and Narration
Oedipus Rex (pp. 704–47): with particular attention to exposition, retrospection, reported action, and choric commentary as means of unfolding

the ironic plot, bringing about the discovery and climax, and mediating the significance of the total action.

The Stronger (pp. 1029–33): with particular attention to retrospection as the means of unfolding the ironic plot, bringing about the discovery and climax, and embodying the significance of the total action.

Drama and Meditation

Everyman (pp. 789–813): with particular attention to the soliloquies of Everyman and the actions and utterances of the other allegorical characters as means of dramatizing a mental and spiritual transformation.

Krapp's Last Tape (pp. 1256–63): with particular attention to the disjointed sequence of memories on the tape, and the reactions of Krapp to the memories, attitudes, and feelings of his earlier self.

Drama and Persuasion

Lysistrata (pp. 750–86): with particular attention to both the verbal and physical conflict between the women and men as means of dramatizing the conflict of values between marital love and political honor.

The Misanthrope (pp. 914–64): with particular attention to the conflict of Alceste with both Philinte and Célimène as a means of dramatizing the conflict of values between social conformity and personal integrity.

Major Barbara (pp. 1035–1103): with particular attention to the conflicts between Undershaft and Lady Britomart, Undershaft and Barbara, Undershaft and Cusins, Undershaft and Stephen, as means of dramatizing the conflict between various economic and social systems.

The Threepenny Opera (pp. 1104–65): with particular attention to the acquisitive and mercenary behavior of all the characters in the play, as well as to the attitudes and values they reflect in their songs, as a means of dramatizing the moral and social consequences of capitalism.

These classifications are not, of course, meant to be prescriptive but only suggestive; they are meant to indicate major elements rather than dominant or exclusive qualities. Indeed, as you lead your students through this sequence of plays, you might gradually encourage them to note the blending of different elements and forms with the ones you are emphasizing in each case. *The Stronger*, for example, might also be seen as having meditative qualities, and *Everyman* might be studied for its persuasive aspects. For similar reasons you might wish to conclude this approach by assigning one of the collected plays that we have not included in these classifications: *Othello* (pp. 817–911); *A Doll's House* (969–1028); *Cat on a Hot Tin Roof* (pp. 1173–1255); or *Mother and Child* (pp. 1166–72). Each play embodies so complex a synthesis of elements from two or three of the literary forms that it defies classification. Thus, any one of them will give your students the opportunity to witness a richly dramatic interaction of the various literary elements and qualities.

The modal—or generic—approach is one of the most widely used methods of teaching drama, not only because it is based on long-standing critical precedents—precedents that reach all the way back to Aristotle's *Poetics*— but also because it provides students with a critical system for understanding the dominant experience of a play and the major elements that create it. Thus we have devoted the longest section in our critical apparatus to this approach. And in that section—"Modes of Drama" (pp. 685–94)—we have not limited our discussion to tragedy and comedy, as is the case in other introductory literature anthologies. We have also included commentary on the other basic modes—satire and romance—that are manifest in drama, as well as on the mixed modes—tragicomedy, naturalism, and the absurdist drama—that seem to prevail in so many modern and contemporary plays. With this material you will be able to give your students a comprehensive, flexible, and critically appropriate approach to the modes of drama. Your students, in turn, will not be forced to pigeon-hole every play they read under the category of tragedy or comedy. They will instead be able to take a tactful approach which recognizes and understands the wide range of experience that drama can imitate and create.

Our collection of plays has likewise been designed to give you a choice among several different ways to teach modes of drama. To assure you that choice we have included at least one play in each of the basic modes, as well as one in each of the important mixed modes. While representing the full range of modes, we have also emphasized the major genres both in traditional and modern drama. Thus our collection gives special emphasis to tragedy, comedy, and naturalistic drama. Here, then, is a classification of the plays, with references to appropriate readings in the critical apparatus and the prefatory notes.

Tragedy
Oedipus Rex, pp. 704–47
"Tragedy and Comedy," pp. 687–90
"Tragedy in the Classical Greek Theater," pp. 701–3

Othello, pp. 817–911
"Tragedy and Comedy," pp. 687–90
"Tragedy in the Renaissance English Theater," pp. 814–16

Comedy
Lysistrata, pp. 750–86
"Tragedy and Comedy," pp. 687–90
"Comedy in the Classical Greek Theater," pp. 748–49

Major Barbara, pp. 1035–1103
"Tragedy and Comedy," pp. 687–90
"Setting and Symbolism in Modern and Contemporary Drama," pp. 965–68

Satire
The Misanthrope, pp. 914–64
"Satire and Romance," pp. 690–92
"Satire on the Neoclassical Stage," pp. 912–13

The Threepenny Opera, pp. 1104–65
"Satire and Romance," pp. 690–92
"Setting and Symbolism in Modern and Contemporary Drama," pp. 965–68

Romance
Everyman, pp. 789–813
"Satire and Romance," pp. 690–92
"Morality Drama on the Medieval Stage," pp. 787–88

Tragicomedy: Naturalistic Drama
A Doll's House, pp. 969–1028
"Tragicomedy, Naturalism, and Absurdist Drama," pp. 692–94
"Setting and Symbolism in Modern and Contemporary Drama," pp. 965–68
The Stronger, pp. 1029–33
"Tragicomedy, Naturalism, and Absurdist Drama," pp. 692–94
"Setting and Symbolism in Modern and Contemporary Drama," pp. 965–68

Cat on a Hot Tin Roof, pp. 1173–1255
"Tragicomedy, Naturalism, and Absurdist Drama," pp. 692–94
"Setting and Symbolism in Modern and Contemporary Drama," pp. 965–68

Mother and Child, pp. 1166–72
"Tragicomedy, Naturalism, and Absurdist Drama," pp. 692–94
"Setting and Symbolism in Modern and Contemporary Drama," pp. 965–68

Tragicomedy: Absurdist Drama
Krapp's Last Tape, pp. 1256–63
"Tragicomedy, Naturalism, and Absurdist Drama," pp. 692–94
"Setting and Symbolism in Modern and Contemporary Drama," pp. 965–68

Using this set of classifications you can organize several different ways of teaching the modes of drama simply by choosing five or six plays from the collection. You might, for example, offer a broad survey of all the modes, in which case you can teach one play from each of the basic modes, and one from each of the mixed modes. Or you might prefer to focus exclusively on the basic modes, in which case you can teach both of the tragedies and comedies, as well as the satire and romance. Or you might prefer to do a sequence on tragedy, comedy, and tragicomedy, in which case you can emphasize either the basic modes or the mixed modes. Or you can focus exclusively on the mixed modes and offer an intensive study of modern tragicomedy. No matter which emphasis you choose, we suggest that you begin by assigning your students pages 685–

87 in the apparatus, "Drama, the World, and Imitation," for this section will give them a synoptic introduction to the modes of drama.

ELEMENTS OF DRAMA

This approach is based on the assumption that students can most easily and effectively be led to an understanding of the whole work by focusing on the basic elements of which it is composed. In the case of drama the basic elements are dialogue, plot, and character. Each of these elements is discussed in our critical apparatus, on pages 645–700. Thus, if you take this approach, you can introduce it by having your students read this section, for it contains not only definitions of the elements, but also detailed methods of examining and understanding them—methods that are specific enough to be useful, yet flexible enough to suit a wide variety of plays.

The elements of drama do not, of course, operate separately from one another, although students might wish that they did, if only to simplify the complex problems of analyzing drama. These problems often appear overwhelming to beginning students of drama, particularly when they are confronted with lengthy plays, containing numerous characters and elaborate plots. To circumvent these problems and help your students develop confidence with this approach, we suggest that you start by having them read a play limited in scope and complexity—a play brief enough that they can read it quickly and comprehend fully the nature and interaction of its dialogue, plot, and characters. For this reason we have included in our collection Strindberg's short one-act play, *The Stronger* (pp. 1029–33).

Strindberg's play contains only two principal characters, Mrs. X and Miss Y, and one minor character, a waitress. Mrs. X is the only one who speaks throughout the entire play, while Miss Y looks on, gazes occasionally at Mrs. X, and laughs once or twice. Yet the play clearly has a plot, which your students will quickly be able to identify as consisting of Mrs. X's change from ignorance to knowledge about her husband's past affair with Miss Y. And they will quickly recognize, too, that the plot is created exclusively out of the interaction between Mrs. X's dialogue and Miss Y's silence—an interaction which also reveals the distinctly different personality of each woman. Thus your students will be able to develop an immediate understanding of the elements and of how they work together to create the experience of drama.

Once your students have developed a basic understanding of the elements within the scope of a very brief and relatively simple play, you can then lead them gradually to study longer and more complex works. Thus before studying a full-length play, you might assign a somewhat longer play, such as *Krapp's Last Tape*, which also entails only a single speaking character. Then you might invite your students to compare the ways that each play creates dramatic tension and interest within the constraints of an apparently very restricted theatrical situation. Both of these plays also involve characters looking back upon their past experiences with a confident sense of understanding which is finally shown to be seriously flawed. Thus you might follow them with a study of *Oedipus Rex*, given the retrospective activity that dominates its ironic plot, inviting your students to compare the ironic plots in each play and to consider what these plots imply in each case about the nature of ignorance and the limits of reason.

Other plays concerned with the problem of knowing—whose central characters undergo an ironic experience, a reversal of fortune, that leads them from ignorance to knowledge—have also been included in our collection, so that you will have a thematically *and* formally related set of works with which to extend and complete this approach to the study of drama. Thus you might follow *Oedipus Rex* with a study of *Everyman* (pp. 789–813), *Othello* (pp. 817–911), and *A Doll's House* (pp. 969–1028). This sequence will also give your students an experience of plays from different historical periods, in a variety of different modes.

Using this sequence you can gradually lead your class to study the elements within the context of comprehensive dramatic purposes that determine the nature of dialogue, plot, and character in any particular play. To this end you might assign our critical section on "Modes of Drama" (pp. 685–94), for it discusses the distinctive handling of the elements in each of the different modes—tragedy, comedy, satire, romance, and tragicomedy.

APPROACHES TO TEACHING PLAYS IN THE COLLECTION

In this section you will find some ideas for teaching each of the plays in our collection—ideas that we have found useful in our own classrooms. Our comments are meant to be suggestive rather than exhaustive. Thus you will not find descriptions of every possible approach to each of the plays. But you will find ideas for dealing with some of the major elements, issues, and problems in each of the plays—issues and problems that are likely to be on the minds of your students when they come to discuss the plays in class. Here, then, are some ideas that will suplement our previous suggestions to teaching drama.

SOPHOCLES, *Oedipus Rex* (pp. 704–47)

Students are perennially disturbed by the apparent injustice of Oedipus's catastrophe. He seems to be the victim of an inescapable fate, one that he is powerless to prevent. Indeed, his righteous desire to rid the city of the Plague—a desire he fulfills during the course of the play—brings him to his final misery. Thus students often consider the play to be not merely ironic, but absurdly unjust, in its outcome. Why should a man of noble achievements and intentions be subjected to the disaster he suffers?

Some answers to this question can be gathered by examining the crucial events in Oedipus's life prior to the action of the play. These events are recalled by Oedipus during the course of his initial conversation with Iokastê, and students should be encouraged to explore their implications, particularly in relation to the character and fate of Oedipus. For example, Oedipus reports that when still a young man—living in Corinth with Polybus and Merope, whom he thought to be his parents—he was told by an oracle that he would kill his father and marry his mother. He recalls, furthermore, that in response to that oracle he fled Corinth, vowing never to see Polybus and Merope again—a reasonable action (students will feel), especially given his equally reasonable assumption that Polybus and Merope were his parents.

But his decisive action in this case—as in other events of his life—might also be viewed as the expedient of an overly rational man, a man not given to exploring the psychological, ethical, and metaphysical implications of the oracle's words or of his own deeds. Oedipus might instead have regarded the oracle's prediction as revealing dreadful aspects of his character, which he was then ignorant of. Thus he might have explored his own character, so as to discover any personal flaws that could possibly lead him to commit such horrible deeds as the oracle predicted. But he ignored these psychological and ethical problems by the physical expedient of running from Polybus and Merope—and thus from himself. His action, then, might be judged as being at once reasonable, but impulsive and evasive; at once ethical in its intent, but ethically blind in its execution, its implications, and its effects.

To what extent can Oedipus's behavior in this instance be considered a paradigm of his actions in all the crucial events of his life? Is it possible to consider his fate the inescapable consequence of responding to the problematic aspects of experience in hyper-rational terms? Is it possible that Oedipus's fate is the probable, though lamentable, outcome of any man who never looks within himself or beyond himself so as to recognize his human limitations—who looks only at the visible phenomena outside of himself that can be mastered by the power of his rational mind? Students might be invited to consider such questions as these not only through an examination of the pre-play action and the play itself, but also through a close study of the persistent imagery in the play referring to sight and blindness. What does it signify, for example, about Oedipus's conception of knowledge that he scorns Teiresias's assertions because they are the claims of a man who lacks the capacity of visual sight?

ARISTOPHANES, *Lysistrata* (pp. 750–86)

Many of your students, having grown up during the Vietnam War, may be troubled rather than satisfied by the comic mode of *Lysistrata*. They may consider it an inappropriate form of response to a war that was destroying the civilization of Aristophanes's time. And they may also consider the "happy idea" of Lysistrata and her cohorts to be not only farfetched but also intolerably sexist—an impossible and disgusting solution to the problem of war.

As a way of responding to these objections you may find it useful to engage your students in thinking about the nature of comedy, as well as about the purposes of laughter and ridicule. You might ask them, for example, whether the only appropriate reaction to a serious problem is a blatantly and straightforwardly serious condemnation of it? In this connection you might discuss with them the black humor of their own time, and ask them whether they consider Catch 22—which many of them have read or seen in movie and television versions—to be an appropriate response to war.

You might also ask them whether the farfetched solution of Lysistrata is to be taken literally or metaphorically—whether Aristophanes meant it to embody his realistic hope for Athens and Sparta, or to stand for a vision of international peace *and* joyous love which he knew was unattainable. Is it possible, then, that just beneath the surface of the play there is a desperate recognition of cultural doom—that Aristophanes's fantasy is only a temporary reprieve which turns out at last to be a painful reminder of the irrievable condition of things? Most comedies contain an element of wish-fulfillment; can this element of fantasy be said to have always a two-edged effect—to be at once an escape from and a reminder of reality?

EVERYMAN (pp. 789–813)

Students may be inclined to dismiss *Everyman* as simply a morality play. They may thus regard it as nothing more than a sermon in dramatic form— a sermon about the spiritual perils of worldliness. It is, admittedly, concerned with inculcating Christian belief in the eternal life of the soul and the temporal life of the body, and it invokes the archetypal fear of death in the service of its religious purpose. This persuasive purpose is announced in the opening speech of the Messenger and summarized in the closing speech of the Doctor. Thus the allegory of the play can be studied as a form of dramatic persuasion.

Yet the persistent capacity of the play to move readers, no matter what the nature of their beliefs—or disbeliefs—must be accounted for by something that transcends its religious purpose. And that "something," of course, is the universal experience of death which is dramatized by its characters and plot. Thus if you approach the play as a dramatization of the mental process that a typical human—Everyman—goes through during the process of dying, your students will find it to be a compelling work, one that exhibits an arresting correspondence to modern psychological studies of death and dying.

In this connection you might read your students passages from Elisabeth Kübler-Ross's book-length study of death and dying, in which she defines the typical stages that people go through when faced with the knowledge of their imminent death—the initial denial of it, the desire to postpone it, the attempt to bargain for its delay, the gradual acceptance of it, and the ultimate yearning for it. Then ask your students to see if they can find analogies to these stages in the experience of Everyman.

Everyman does, in fact, go through a comparable mental process, and each stage of his experience is not only clearly marked out but also psychologically developed so as to have dramatic plausibility. Near the end of the play, for example, Everyman is so taken up with the busyness of receiving the final sacrament that he momentarily overlooks the fact that in dying he will not only give up his bodily existence but will also lose his "Five Wits"—his sensory awareness, his consciousness of being in the world. That inevitable loss of consciousness is very easy to overlook, even for those who like Everyman have acknowledged the inevitability of death, for it is at last very difficult to conceive of the absence of consciousness, much less to accept it. In this psychological detail, as in others, *Everyman* will sustain the close examination of your students.

For other dramatic studies of death and dying, students might be invited to examine and compare the behavior of Dr. Rank in *A Doll's House*, as well as that of Big Daddy in *Cat on a Hot Tin Roof*. Along the same line of analysis, you might invite students to examine how friends and relatives respond to a dying person. How do Fellowship, Kindred, and Cousin respond to Everyman when they learn of his imminent death? How do Nora and Torvald respond to Dr. Rank when they learn of his imminent death? How do Big Daddy's wife and children respond to him when they learn of his imminent death? Is there a reciprocal psychological process that friends and relatives go through in response to the mental process of the dying person?

SHAKESPEARE, *Othello* (pp. 817–911)

Problems of motivation and probability abound in *Othello,* and the problems are not limited simply to accounting for the pivotal effect of the missing handkerchief. The first problem that students might be faced with is that of accounting for Iago's motivation. He appears initially to be moved simply by envy of Cassio for his promotion to lieutenant, but in his soliloquies he subsequently professes to be jealous of Othello for his marriage to Desdemona, as well as to desire vengeance on Othello for the mere suspicion of having been cuckolded by him. Iago's motivation thus seems inconstant and inconsistent. In fact, the only constant element in Iago's motivation is his professed hatred of Othello—a hatred that Iago never actually accounts for in his soliloquies. Is it possible that Iago's motive is at last so irrational and inexplicable that it is unknown even to him? Or is it the case that his motive is implicit in his repeatedly contemptuous references to Othello's goodness? Is Othello's goodness an intolerable condition for Iago to behold, given an acute sense of his own imperfection? Or is Iago's behavior a case of motiveless malignancy?

A similar set of questions might be raised about Othello's motivation and behavior. How can a character of such heroic proportions—so resourceful in war and in love, so self-disciplined during the turmoil of the first two acts—become so quickly and easily unstrung during the last three acts by the insinuations of Iago? Why does he repose so much trust in Iago, having previously judged him less deserving than Cassio? Why does he rely so heavily on "ocular proof" and so little on his intuitive knowledge of Desdemona's character (in this respect he is arrestingly similar to Oedipus)? And why does he finally murder Desdemona? Because he is "Perplexed in the extreme" by jealousy? Or because he sees himself as a minister of justice, and thus compelled to kill her "else she'll betray more men"? And why, having murdered her, does he initially seek to conceal the deed from Emilia? How can a character so innately good—not only in his own eyes but in the eyes of others—be driven to such evil deeds? Is there an unspecified weakness in his moral character? Or is he at last the victim of a literal-minded—and thus illusory—conception of truth and honesty (and in this respect also similar to Oedipus)?

For another play dealing with the experience of jealousy and the problematic nature of truth and honesty, students might be invited to read and compare *The Misanthrope*.

MOLIÈRE, *The Misanthrope* (pp. 914–64)

The opening scene of this play immediately provokes readers to take sides, some preferring the moral integrity of Alceste, others espousing the social awareness of Philinte. Indeed, you will probably find that this quarrel between Alceste and Philinte is so provocative, arouses such deeply felt allegiances, that your students will start quarreling about it with one another during the first day you discuss the play in class. And if they do not start quarreling on their own, you should have little trouble provoking them to do so. As you can see, we believe in arousing disagreement about the central issue of the play, because the play itself is designed to arouse disagreement.

But is the play designed to resolve that disagreement in favor of one side or the other? This is the central problem that your students must finally face up to, and they can only deal with it by examining the events and the plot of the play. The traditional view is that Philinte is to be regarded as the voice of reason, of common sense, of a necessary social awareness; yet these undeniable virtues often lead him to tolerate the legal and moral corruptions of his society. Alceste, of course, is unremittingly true to his word and to his moral beliefs; and yet his consequent misanthropy turns out to be intolerant and intolerable. Is it possible, then, that the play is meant to leave readers confused about their allegiances? Is it possible that Molière means to imply that the conflict of values cannot be resolved?

The final scene of the play is suggestive in this respect. It presents a dubious engagement between Philinte and Eliante, as well as a stalemate between Alceste and Célimène, as if to imply that no one gains the upper hand at the end. And the final words of Philinte indicate his immediate intention to buttonhole Alceste, to mollify his rage, an intention that might well lead to another quarrel exactly like the one at the beginning of the play. Thus the plot of the play—like the argument of its central characters—seems to be circular and unending. As a means of pointing up the ironic effect of this final scene, you might have your students read and compare the festive and harmonious conclusions of both *Lysistrata* and *Major Barbara*.

HENRIK IBSEN, *A Doll's House* (pp. 969–1028)

The currently popular view of the play is that it embodies a condemnation of male chauvinism and an affirmation of woman's rights. And there is much about the relationship of Torvald and Nora that supports this interpretation, not the least of which is his nearly total subjugation and humiliation of her—his conception of her as his "little songbird" and "doll"—as well as her final rejection of his belief that she must be "First and foremost . . . a wife and mother," and her consequent decision to "think things out for myself, and try to find my own answer."

But it is also appropriate to balance this view for your students with Ibsen's own statements about the play:

> I . . . must disclaim the honor of having consciously worked for women's rights. I am not even quite sure what women's rights really are. To me it has been a question of human rights.

Ibsen's statement is, in fact, an echo of Nora's assertion that "I am first and foremost a human being." That belief leads her at last to leave Torvald not because he has subjugated her, but because he has profoundly disappointed her by valuing his material welfare and social status more highly than her human love. Thus she no longer loves him, because he is not the man she thought him to be, not the man she hoped him to be, not the man she "could share my life with." The implications of these remarks seems to be that she could have forgiven him everything had he finally been true to her hopeful vision of him. Thus her departure might well be seen as the logical consequence of her shattered illusion.

The entire play seems, in fact, to be concerned with the human devastation that is wrought by clinging to illusions—not only about marriage, but about any personal relationship, indeed about life and death as well. In this connection it might be profitable to have your students consider the character, behavior, and function of Dr. Rank. Though he hovers over the entire play, much as he hovers over the lives of Nora and Torvald, he is rarely discussed by critics, instructors, or students. Is he present in the play simply to expose the emotional naïveté of Nora and the callousness of Torvald? Or is his clinically unflinching attention to his impending death meant to epitomize the ideal of living—and dying—without illusions? And is it, perhaps, the courage of Rank that inspires Nora to shed her own illusions?

AUGUST STRINDBERG, *The Stronger* (pp. 1029–33)

The title of the play and the concluding dialogue of Mrs. X clearly raise the question of which woman is "the stronger." But an equally fascinating question—which must be answered prior to the other—concerns the nature of strength itself. Does strength refer to psychological power in a struggle of wills? Is it manifested by gaining the upper hand in an emotional and sexual triangle? Or is strength to be equated with psychological self-sufficiency? Or is it, instead, to be seen as inseparable from knowledge—not only of oneself but of others? Which of the women knows more in this play? And how do we know?

No matter how your students interpret the idea of strength embodied in the play, they will still be left with the problem of gathering reliable information about the character, the past behavior, the past relationships, the present relationships, and the present situation of both women, particularly Miss Y. To do so your students will have to examine Mrs. X's dialogue meticulously, sifting truth from half-truth, from falsehood. And they will have to examine carefully Miss Y's gestures and facial expressions, noting the exact point in Mrs. X's dialogue at which each of those gestures and expressions occurs.

This is also implicitly a play about theater, for both main characters are actresses, though presumably neither one is any longer employed. What view of theatrical life does it seem to imply? And which of the women is the better actress?

GEORGE BERNARD SHAW, *Major Barbara* (pp. 1035–1103)

Though Barbara is the title character of the play, Undershaft is self-evidently Shaw's spokesman and protagonist, challenging as he does the aristocratic socioeconomic system avowed by Lady Britomart and Stephen, as well as the Salvation Army method of social welfare practiced by Barbara, and opposing them with his capitalistic vision of social progress. Undershaft's conversion of everyone through his dazzling wit and the utopian spectacle of his model working community will no doubt trouble, or at least puzzle, many students, even those who subscribe completely to his capitalistic outlook, given the fact that it is allied to the seemingly diabolical morality of the munitions manufacturer. Students will wonder, quite simply, whether or not Shaw endorses everything espoused by Undershaft, given the fact that Undershaft has the upper hand and the last word on every issue in the play.

In order to set the record straight about Shaw's socioeconomic views, it might be useful to tell students that he was, in fact, an active member of the Fabians, a socialist group that was influenced by the theories of Karl Marx, but that did not regard the state as a class structure to be overthrown, so much as social mechanism to be gradually altered and used for the promotion of public welfare. Thus they will recognize that Shaw could hardly have subscribed to Undershaft's capitalistic vision, much less to his armorer's morality. Still, they might well wonder why Shaw would create a hero whose views were apparently so opposed to his own. In order to resolve this problem, it will be necessary to inform students that Shaw typically created his heroes and heroines out of highly implausible figures, and typically endowed them with outlandish, or at least provocative, ideas, because he wanted to shock his audience out of their conventional attitudes about morality, society, and politics, and because he believed that the "free vitality" of "liberated thought" was the only sure way of working a "creative evolution" in the human condition. With this background, students will be able to see that Shaw's attitude toward Undershaft is more complex than it might seem at first glance.

Perhaps the most effective means of helping students to understand the outlook of the play will be to have them examine it in the context of its subtitle, "A Discussion in Three Acts," which clearly suggests that the play is structured very much like a debate—a contest among various socioeconomic views and among the persons who hold those views. Once the plot is seen as being structured like a debate, it will be possible to show students that Undershaft is by no means the immoral character he appears to be, but rather that he regards the politics of Stephen, the morality of Barbara, and the intelligence of Cusins as being helpless to improve the human condition without the authentic power he possesses. At the same time, it will be possible to show students that Undershaft also recognizes true progress as requiring the moral and intelligent exercise of power, which is why he vies so energetically for the allegiance of Barbara and Cusins. Given this view of plot, it should be possible for students to see that Undershaft does not actually win the debate outright, that the play actually works very much like a dialectical process. Accordingly, the thesis of Barbara and Cusins is challenged by the antithesis of Undershaft, and the result is a synthesis of views, reflected in the comic resolution which unites all the central characters, young and old, through the settling of the inheritance and the promise of a marriage that signals the formation of a new social order.

Shaw's comic synthesis of opposing socioeconomic views might well be compared to the classical pattern of a comic plot in *Lysistrata*. Shaw's social optimism, especially as it is reflected in Undershaft's capitalistic utopianizing, deserves to be balanced by Brecht's satiric view of capitalism in *The Threepenny Opera*. And the enduring relevance of Shaw's concerns, particularly as they are embodied in the debate between Barbara and Undershaft, might well be established by pointing to the continuing debate in American political life between liberal and conservative approaches to economic and social policy.

BERTOLT BRECHT, *The Threepenny Opera* (pp. 1104–65)

Brecht's biting attack on capitalism is so pointed and explicit that students should have little trouble in recognizing the dominant satiric purpose of *The Threepenny Opera*. Just to make certain, however, that they do recognize this overriding purpose and the various ways in which it is expressed, you might find it useful to have them review the various characters and their activities throughout the play, with an eye to noticing that everyone in this sleazy world, including Polly, is driven by a lust for money—a lust so consuming that it knows no moral limits, and thus turns all of the characters into predators. They should see, for example, that the theme of capitalistic exploitation is announced in the opening scene at Peachum's outfitting shop for beggars, which vividly depicts the cynical enterprise of a businessman who thrives on poverty. They should see, in turn, that Peachum's pack of beggars is matched by Macheath's gang of thieves, whose female counterparts are to be found in Jenny and the Turnbridge whores. Above all, they should see that the world of Brecht's play is not like that of Robin Hood and his merry thieves, who steal from the rich in order to sustain the poor—that in Brecht's capitalistic jungle there is no honor among thieves. More to the point, there are no human ties, whether of family, friendship, or love, that transcend the craving for money. Thus the Peachums are willing to exploit their daughter Polly, and the whores are willing to exploit Macheath, and Macheath is willing to exploit his fellow thieves, in what appears to be an endless round of buying and selling. And this craven spectacle is repeatedly echoed in the songs, which declare, for example, that "money rules the world," that law is "made for one thing alone, for the exploitation of those who don't understand it," and that "Mankind can keep alive thanks to its brilliance in keeping its humanity repressed."

While students will probably be quick to recognize these political and economic dimensions of the satire, they may not readily see that Brecht is also mocking romantic ideas of love, exemplified in Polly's naive attachment to the lusty Macheath, who "even with all London at his heels . . . is not the man to give up his habits"—or his whores. Students will probably also need help in recognizing that Brecht is likewise deriding traditional opera through the bitter lyrics and dissonant cabaret music that figure in *The Threepenny Opera*. Given his grim view of romantic love, of course, it is hardly surprising that Brecht inverts all the conventions of grand opera. Ultimately, however, even these satiric targets are not separable from his assault on capitalistic society, for that assault encompasses every aspect of capitalism as it is perceived by Brecht—from its ethics and its politics to its idea of love and its standards of art. In the range of his satire, as in its form, Brecht was inspired, of course, by *The Beggar's Opera* of John Gay, and it might be useful to tell students about his source, so that they can appreciate the genius of Brecht in adapting it to his own cultural vision. Brecht, for example, drew all of his characters and much of his plot from Gay's work, but in virtually every case he altered details to create a much more savage view of the world, as can be seen simply by comparing the Robin Hood quality of Macheath in Gay's work with Brecht's acknowledged conception of him as an emblem of bourgeois cynicism.

Probably the most effective way of helping students to experience and understand the harshness of Brecht's satire will be to bring in a recording of the work, so that they can hear the dissonant and haunting music of Kurt Weill, which repeatedly heightens the jarring and jangling quality of the lyrics and of the constantly shifting spectacle that takes place from scene to scene. And in this context, of course, it will be useful to discuss Brecht's radical approach to drama, namely "epic theater," which is explained in the headnote on Brecht immediately preceding the text of the work.

Brecht's satiric view of capitalism deserves to be balanced by Undershaft's view of it in *Major Barbara*. The epic theater of Brecht's satire might profitably be compared to the classical satiric methods of Aristophanes, combining as they both do not only character, plot, and dialogue, but also songs and music. Brecht deliberately intended "epic theater" as a challenge to the naturalistic methods of such dramatists as Ibsen and Strindberg, and for this reason *The Threepenny Opera* might be systematically contrasted with the theatrical style of *A Doll's House*. Brecht's view of the businessman as it is portrayed in Peachum might also be compared to Ibsen's view as it is represented by Torvald, as well as to Williams's as it is embodied in Big Daddy.

LANGSTON HUGHES, *Mother and Child* (pp. 1166–72)

Mother and Child is a very dramatic little work that achieves its effects by means of a highly unusual and ingenious strategy—specifically, by creating a set of characters who are nominally the center of interest in the play—the mother and child, the husband and Douglass—but who never appear in the play itself. Given the fact that these four characters are of such consuming interest to the personages who actually appear in the play—the members of the Salvation Rock Missionary Society—your students may be equally interested in speculating about the behavior of these absent characters and about the potential effects of their behavior on the local community. But Hughes, of course, is less interested in the nominally central characters than in what the gossipy discussion about them reveals of the social and cultural attitudes that are held by the various women who belong to the Missionary Society.

Once you have led students to recognize the actual focus of the play, you might then invite them to examine the various women who belong to the Society, with an eye to describing, comparing, and contrasting their several reactions to the mother and child, the husband and Douglass. Then you might have students examine the women's varying attitudes and feelings about the various racial issues in the community—about past, present, and future relationships between whites and blacks. Given the fact that the women belong to a Christian Missionary Society, it might be appropriate to have students consider which of the women are most Christian in their attitudes and reactions, and which are least Christian in their behavior. In this context, students might also be invited to consider the implications and effects of the various religious expressions, exclamations, and utterances that are made in the play, not to mention the hymn with which the play concludes, and the title of the play itself. Finally, of course, you might want to have students pull together all of their observations by reflecting upon what the play seems to imply about the causes and nature of racial conflict.

For another perspective on *Mother and Child,* you might have students read and examine it in relation to Strindberg's *The Stronger,* since both are relatively short plays, and both involve extensive discussion of characters who do not appear in the play, yet are evidently of central interest in the play. Given this formal similarity, you might invite students to describe and explain how dramatic conflict, interaction, and resolution are created out of situations that appear to be inherently undramatic, if only because they consist exclusively of gossip and other conventional forms of conversation.

TENNESSEE WILLIAMS, *Cat on a Hot Tin Roof* (pp. 1173–1255)

A recurring topic of dialogue is Brick's past relationship with Skipper. Everyone in the play suspects—or believes—the relationship to have been homosexual, either latently or literally, on Brick's part, or on Skipper's part, or on the part of both. Thus you should not be surprised if your students also focus on that relationship and attempt to determine its exact identity. The problem, of course, is that it cannot be verified one way or another. And even if it could be substantiated—or disproved—we would still not be able to account for Brick's all-consuming malaise and paralysis. Nor, for that matter, would it help us to explain the behavior of any of the other characters in the play. Thus you should probably try to dissuade your students from making too much of the relationship, lest it distract them from more central issues in the play.

One of the central problems, of course, is to account for the painful sense of dissatisfaction that pervades all the characters and all their intimate relationships with one another. From its opening to its closing scene, in fact, the play repeatedly bears witness to a psychological war that has been going on for years among all the members of the family. As a result of that conflict, every one of the characters has taken part in a betrayal of trust, a manipulation of affections, or some form of psychological "mendacity," as Brick calls it at the end of the second act. And the mendacity persists throughout the play, in spite of—or, perhaps, because of—the family crisis that is provoked by Big Daddy's fatal illness. The action of the play, indeed, is occasioned by his illness—a circumstance suggesting that perhaps Big Daddy himself is the cause of everyone's misery. He does, after all, exert a profound psychic influence on all the characters and all their marriages—including his own. Is it possible, then, that Big Daddy—and not Brick or Margaret—is the central character of the play?

Is it possible that the affections, the inclinations, and the relations of all the characters are diseased by his influence? Or, to put the matter in another context, is it possible that the cancer from which he suffers—that invisible disease destroying him from within—is to be taken as a metaphor for the malignant quality of his influence upon the members of his family? You might consider this question with your students by inviting them to identify the precise effect that Big Daddy has on each of the characters and each of the marriages portrayed in the play.

SAMUEL BECKETT, *Krapp's Last Tape* (pp. 1256–63)

The bizarre physical makeup of Krapp, as well as his bizarre physical and mental activities, will, no doubt fascinate and puzzle your students. And in order to account for his behavior, they may well be inclined to regard him as a symbol—an embodiment—of failed humanity perhaps, or of mental disturbance, or of aged infirmity, or of various other depressing and unfortunate conditions suggested by the strange activities that absorb him throughout the play. But before they leap to these easy, and rather literal, interpretations, it might be appropriate to have them examine his activity in detail.

The dominant activity of the play, of course, is Krapp's listening to the autobiographical tape he made on his thirty-ninth birthday. But in order for students to understand this activity, they will have to see it in the context of Krapp's lifelong obsession with making a tape-recorded journal of his life. Thus it might be useful to begin this discussion by inviting students to report all of the facts they can discover about Krapp's tape collection and the habitual activities he performs in maintaining and recording his taped autobiography. In order to do so, they will have to examine not only the stage directions, but also the tape, as well as Krapp's intermittent reactions to the tape, and Krapp's statements on the tape that he begins recording near the end of the play. By gathering information from these various sources, they should discover that Krapp apparently makes a tape each year on his birthday, in which he reviews the previous year of his life, and that he has been doing so since at least the age of twenty-seven. They should also recognize that all of the tapes are apparently kept in numbered boxes, which in turn are indexed and briefly identified with notations about their contents in a written ledger. They should also recognize that whenever Krapp is about to record his experiences each year, he apparently reviews tapes from preceding years, so that he is continually in the process of reviewing and re-reviewing his previous life, and his tapes are thus a record not only of his experiences for a given year, but also of his reactions to the feelings, thoughts, and desires that have moved in him in earlier years.

Once students have put together all of this information, they should be able to see that all the activity of the play is, in fact, leading up to the consummation of Krapp's annual birthday ritual—the recording of the tape for his sixty-ninth birthday—which he begins in his last piece of extended dialogue, but does not complete, preferring instead to listen again to a segment from the tape for his thirty-ninth birthday. Given the compelling interest this tape seems to have for Krapp, it might well be made the focus of yet another information-gathering project for students. In this case, you might invite them to make an index of all the topics and experiences, thoughts and feelings, that are discussed on the tape, as well as the relative amount of time and attention that is given to each of the subjects. Having gathered this information, students should discover that though the tape covers a wide variety of topics, ranging from Krapp's insatiable appetite for bananas to his intellectual aspirations and spiritual hopes, it focuses on the quality of his emotional and sexual life. This preoccupation is evident from the numerous women who figure in the taped memories, ranging from Old Miss McGlome and Krapp's dying mother to all of the younger women whom he has either eyed on the street or become involved with in passing sexual encounters.

Having led students to perceive the dominant orientation in the tape itself, you might then invite them to examine Krapp's reactions to the tape, which are evident not only in his intermittent bits of dialogue while listening to the tape, but also in the segments of the tape he chooses to listen to during his initial playback of it, and in the segment he chooses to replay at the end, as well as in the statements he makes about it at the beginning of his tape for the sixty-ninth year. This analysis will reveal that though Krapp scorns his earlier emotional and sexual involvements, much as he had thirty-nine years earlier, he is inescapably drawn back to them in a poignantly reflexive movement of mind. Thus the action of the play paradoxically shows a man who is at once obsessively self-absorbed and yet hungering for the love of another human being, a man whose clownish appearance ("White face. Purple nose") and slapstick craving for bananas are ultimately balanced by his undying emotional needs.

Given his tape recorder and tape collection, his autobiographical and auto-analytical preoccupations, his gastro-intestinal and sexual hangups, his banana and soda-pop binges, Krapp is very much like a modern-day everyman. Indeed, the play itself might fruitfully be compared to the medieval *Everyman,* since both works are examples of meditative drama, representing as they do the mental activity of typical human beings looking back upon their lives, attempting to find meaning and value in what they have done and believed. In this context, you might also invite students to examine and compare Big Daddy's extended review of his life in Act 2 of *Cat on a Hot Tin Roof.* For a different perspective on *Krapp's Last Tape,* you might have students read and discuss it in relation to Strindberg's *The Stronger,* since both are relatively short plays, each of which is distinguished by the fact that it contains only a single speaking character. Given this similar constraint, you might invite students to describe and explain how each play develops dramatic conflict and interaction out of a theatrical limitation that might appear to deny the possibility of conflict and interaction.

Essay

CARL H. KLAUS

WHY THE ESSAY?

That question—or some form of it—may well be on your mind as you think about using our anthology, so we'd like to answer it right off. Though most other introductory literature anthologies exclude the essay, we have included it, and we have done so for several reasons. To begin with, we consider the essay to be a form of literature that is interesting in its own right. Like fiction, poetry, and drama, the essay uses language and, like those other forms, it often uses language very imaginatively. Because of its intrinsic literary merit, the essay has, we believe, a rightful place in our anthology. We can see no reason to discriminate against essays such as Swift's *A Modest Proposal*, Orwell's *Shooting an Elephant*, or Woolf's *The Death of the Moth*. The world of the literary essay, after all, includes a wealth of rich pieces such as those, pieces that your students deserve to lay their hands on; and we have tried to make some of those riches accessible to your students—and to you—in our collection of essays. Thus you will find those acknowledged masterpieces in our collection, as well as equally challenging literary essays by contemporary writers such as Norman Mailer, Nora Ephron, and Joan Didion.

But beyond the literary excellence of the essay, there are also some very good pedagogical reasons for including it in an introduction to literature. The essay, after all, is the literary form most directly concerned with truth, most concerned with convincing us of the version of reality that it presents. This makes the essay an especially appropriate form for beginning the study of literature. Because it is the most direct of the forms, your students will find that it yields the secrets of its structure and its meaning most readily. Thus the essay is a sure way to put your students at ease in the beginning of the course, to help them develop the confidence and the understanding they will need when they turn to the more indirect—and thus more complex—forms of fiction, poetry, and drama.

The essay is also an appropriate form to begin with, because your students already know something—but not everything—about it. Most of your students will be familiar with completely practical forms of the essay, having read them and written them in their freshman or high-school composition courses. But by the same token most of your students will not be familiar with the literary forms of the essay that we have anthologized. Given their past experience with the practical side of the essay, your students will be genuinely surprised to discover the imaginative turns it can take in the hands of literary essayists such as Thoreau, Mark Twain, Forster, Thurber, or White. By exploring with your students the contrast between their past experience of the essay and their experience of it in your course, you will have a natural basis for beginning to discuss with them the difference between utilitarian and literary forms of writing. We have deliberately tried to acknowledge your students' past experience with the essay in our introduction to the essay (pp. 1267–69), and in those opening pages we have even suggested some essays they might read on their own to give them a new and different perception of the form, one that shows them its imaginative, its literary, possibilities.

The astonishing flexibility of the essay—its capacity to assume so many different forms—is perhaps the most compelling reason for including it at the beginning of an introductory literature course. Just as it can range between utilitarian and literary forms, so it can vary from using conventionally persuasive techniques to using narrative, poetic, or even dramatic elements of form. Thus the essay can quite conveniently serve as a preview of the major literary forms—fiction, poetry, and drama—that you will be teaching in your course. To make such a preview possible, we have organized our critical introduction to the essay (pp. 1267–1303) in terms of distinctions between argumentative, narrative, poetic, and dramatic forms of the essay. And we have provided sample essays to illustrate our discussion of each different form. So, within the familiar world of the essay you can begin to prepare your students for the unfamiliar elements of form they will encounter in fiction, poetry, and drama. Our collection, for example, includes essays which you can use to illustrate point of view, tone, and narrative technique in fiction; analogy, metaphor, and conceit in poetry; as well as dialogue, setting, and plot in drama.

Once your students have an initial grasp of the literary forms, they will be better prepared to study each of the forms in greater detail. They will be prepared, too, to recognize that although each form has its unique qualities, each is capable of drawing upon the elements and strategies of the others. We have discussed some of those distinctions and interrelationships among the forms in our general introduction (pp. xxiii–xxvii), but our discussion, of course, cannot take the place of your students' firsthand experience and your classroom discussion of the basic literary forms. And that can most efficiently be prepared for by beginning with a study of the essay. Thus by taking up the essay with your students, you will be able to give them a more spacious, a more properly comprehensive, view of the world of literature than is possible without it.

DESIGN, SCOPE, AND FLEXIBILITY OF THE ESSAY SECTION

In the Essay section of our anthology (pp. 1267–1351), you and your students will find a critical introduction to the essay as a form of literature (pp. 1267–1303), and a collection of literary essays (pp. 1305–51). Our critical section provides a discussion of the basic elements of the essay, of the various literary forms it can take, and of how to analyze each of the forms.

The longest part of the critical section (pp. 1273–1303) is given over to explaining methods of analyzing each form, and there you will find four representative essays with sample analyses of each. For the convenience of you and your students, we have summarized our analytic methods at the end of the critical section, so that they can be used by students when they turn to the collection of essays. As an additional aid to studying essays and writing about them, we have provided a Glossary of Critical Terms at the end of the book.

The collection proper contains thirteen additional essays by major essayists from the eighteenth century through the twentieth. We have arranged these essays chronologically, not only because that order provides the handiest system for locating selections, but also because it will make the fewest critical impositions on your students when they turn to reading, interpreting, and discussing the essays with you in class. For the same reason we have presented the essays in the collection without any comments or questions. The right to make interpretative comments and questions belongs, after all, primarily to you and your students. Thus we have confined our comments and questions to the five essays in our critical section.

Our collection plus our critical section provides a total of seventeen essays—far more material, we realize, than you can possibly use. But in this, as in the other sections of our anthology, we have aimed to produce a collection flexible enough to meet the varying needs of many instructors and students. And flexibility can only be achieved by giving you too much rather than not enough. The size and design of our collection will enable you to choose among a variety of approaches and corresponding essays rather than having a single approach and a limited set of essays imposed upon you. You will have enough essays to assign for class discussion, independent reading, and paper assignments. And your students will still be left with essays to read for their own interest and pleasure.

Given the flexibility of our essay section, your only problem will be to decide which approach to take in teaching the essays, and which essays will best suit your approach. To help you make those decisions is one of our main purposes here. Thus you will find, in the pages that follow, not only comments on each of the individual essays but also an explanation of several different approaches you can take, along with a list of essays that will best suit each approach.

APPROACHES TO TEACHING THE ESSAY

In our own teaching of literature, we have found that selecting an overall approach is the most important decision we can make for ourselves and for our students. Once we have a critical approach in mind, we know where we are going in the course, we have an idea of how to get there, and we can map the course for our students as well. Our critical approach guides us in selecting material, arranging it, and proportioning the time we give to each selection. Thus the choice of an approach influences all the other decisions we make in the planning of a course. We assume that the choice of a guiding approach is equally important to you, and so we have given over this section to information and ideas that will help you to make that decision in connection with the teaching of the essay. The decision, of course, is yours, and thus we will not presume to recommend any one approach as being preferable to the others. Instead, we will simply describe the various possibilities and indicate the essays as well as the portions of our critical section that will work best with each approach.

Two basic types of approach presently appear to prevail in introductory literature courses, and these can be roughly classified as *formal* and *thematic*. Thus we have used these terms as convenient points of reference for organizing this section. Under each of these categories, you will find several different approaches to choose from, as well as a list of appropriate essays and appropriate parts of the critical section for each approach.

FORMAL

1. *A survey of the basic forms of the literary essay, beginning with the most direct and moving systematically to the most indirect—from "argumentative," to "narrative," to "poetic," and finally to the two types of "dramatic" (dialogue and monologue).*

This approach will serve both as a study of the essay and as a preview of the other literary forms. To facilitate this approach, students can be taken step by step through the critical section, from one form to the next, matching readings in the critical section with readings from the collection itself. For example, students can first be assigned pages 1267–79 in the critical section, which include a brief survey of the elements and forms of the literary essay, an introduction to the *argumentative* form, a sample "argumentative" essay by D. H. Lawrence, and a detailed analysis of Lawrence's essay. Once the students have had a chance to read and discuss this material, they can then be assigned an "argumentative" essay from the collection, either for independent reading, for class discussion, or for a written assignment (of analysis or imitation). A similar procedure can be followed for each of the subsequent forms: *narrative* essay, pp. 1279–88; *poetic* essay, pp. 1288–96; *dramatic dialogue*, 1296–1301. And as a review of the several forms, students can be assigned the summary section on pages 1302–3.

Here, then, is a formal classification of the essays which you can use in making appropriate assignments for this approach, as well as for some of the others which follow in this subsection.

Argumentative Essay
SWIFT, "A Modest Proposal" (pp. 1306–13)
CLEAVER, "The Blood Lust" (pp. 1346–48)

GREGORY, "If You Had to Kill Your Own Hog" (pp. 1341–43)
MAILER, "A Statement for *Architectural Forum*" (pp. 1338–40)
THOMAS, "The Iks" (pp. 1336–38)

Narrative Essay
THOREAU, "The War of the Ants" (pp. 1313–16)
ORWELL, "Shooting an Elephant" (pp. 1322–28)
WOOLF, "The Death of the Moth" (pp. 1318–20)
THURBER, "The Moth and the Star" (p. 1321)

Poetic Essay
EISELEY, "The Bird and the Machine" (pp. 1329–35)
DIDION, "On Going Home" (pp. 1343–45)
DILLARD, "Death of a Moth" (pp. 1348–51)

Dramatic Essay
Dialogue   MARK TWAIN, "In the Animals' Court" (pp. 1316–18)

These classifications, by the way, are not in all cases airtight, since some essays, as we note in our critical section, "combine the various possibilities of form in rich and complex ways." Thus the classifications should be used with tact. In this list we have simply categorized the essays according to what appears to us to be the dominant literary form. In our section of comment on individual essays, we have noted any selections that combine elements of more than one form.

Narrative essays, as you can see from this list, bulk largest in our collection, and they do so for several reasons. To begin with, the essay, because of its direct address to the reader, is most closely allied in form to narrative. Thus literary essays tend to use narrative elements more often than elements of the other forms. And we felt that our collection should reflect that tendency. For similar reasons, we also assumed that most instructors would incline to follow the essay with a study of the short story. Thus we have offered a relatively large choice of narrative essays to facilitate that transition. Just the same, the essays in our collection together with those in the critical section provide an adequate representation of the other forms for an introductory study of each.

2. *A study of each form of the literary essay in connection with the major literary form to which it is most closely allied.*
   This approach is a variation on the first, but sufficiently different to be described separately here. In this approach the essay is very heavily subordinated to the study of fiction, poetry, and drama. Instead of systematically surveying all forms of the essay, both for their own interest and for a preview of the other literary forms, this approach uses the essay primarily as an introduction to separate studies of fiction, poetry, and drama.
   If you wish to adopt this approach, you can do so by first assigning

students pages 1267–88 in the critical section, which include a brief survey of the elements and forms of the literary essay, followed by a detailed analysis of Lawrence's "argumentative" essay and of Ephron's "narrative" essay. In taking up this material with students, you might slant your discussion to emphasize the special elements that distinguish Ephron's "narrative" essay—the elements of storytelling, such as her description of characters, reporting of dialogue, and presentation of events. Though Ephron's essay incorporates all of these narrative elements, it also contains an extensive section of commentary in which she interprets her "story." And her story makes no pretense of being about imaginary characters and events. It is explicitly about the cultural significance of actual persons and incidents. Having discussed Ephron's piece as an essay in which narration is explicitly subordinate to persuasion, you might then move on to another "narrative" essay (see our classification in subsection 1 above)—but in this case an essay where commentary is so thoroughly fused with storytelling (as in Woolf's "The Death of the Moth") that it is barely discernible, except at the end, as being a meditation on the mystery and the power of death. Following Woolf's essay, you might turn to a piece of realistic fiction in which the narrator offers no interpretative commentary, one such as Chekhov's "Heartache" (pp. 193–98), and then explore with your students the problem of how meaning is conveyed in fiction.

By following a similar procedure, you can also use the essay as a preparation for the study of poetry. You can begin by assigning your students pages 1288–96 in the critical section, which include an introduction to the "poetic" essay, a sample of that form (E. B. White's "Spring"), and a detailed analysis of White's essay. In taking up this material, you would probably do best to focus on the techniques by which White organizes images in his descriptive sections to prepare for reflections in his meditative sections. Then you might have your students read Annie Dillard's "The Death of a Moth" (pp. 1348–51), in which there is no explicit meditation, even though its images are fraught with meditative implications. Following Dillard's essay you might turn to the discussion of description and meditation in the critical section on poetry (pp. 433–35), and explore with your students the problem of how meaning is conveyed in poetry not only through images but also through their formal organization in verse.

To use the essay as an introduction to drama, you can assign pages 1296–1303 in the critical section, which include an introduction to the essay as "dialogue," an example of that form (E. M. Forster's "Our Graves at Gallipoli"), and an analysis of Forster's essay. In taking up this material, you can easily show your students how Forster uses character, plot, and dialogue to make his argument against war. Following Forster's piece you might have your students read the critical section on persuasive drama (p. 684), then have them read a full-length play against war, such as *Lysistrata* (pp. 750–86), and finally discuss with them the comparative techniques by which each work attempts to make its case. Or instead of *Lysis-*

trata you might assign *The Misanthrope* (pp. 914–64), and then discuss the difference in technique between a dramatic essay which clearly takes a stand on a controversial issue and a full-length play which explores but does not finally resolve a difficult problem of values.

For a quite different but striking approach to drama, you might begin by having your students read Swift's "Modest Proposal" and focus on the techniques by which Swift projects the character of his modest proposer, so as to achieve the ironic effect of his essay. Following Swift's ironic essay, you can then assign a brief ironic play (Strindberg's *The Stronger*, pp. 1029–33), which involves two characters only one of which speaks. Then you might explore with your students the differences in form and technique between Swift's "dramatic monologue" and Strindberg's "monologue drama." You might consider, in particular, how the presence of the silent character in *The Stronger* influences the behavior of the speaking character, so that her monologue becomes more than a prose statement, becomes in fact a play with a fully articulated plot, which includes not only an exposition and development but also a very surprising climax.

In the preceding paragraphs we have discussed some, but by no means all, of the arrangements through which the essay can be used as an introduction to each of the major forms. Our comments have been suggestive rather than exhaustive. Additional assignment sequences can easily be discovered by consulting the formal classification of essays (in subsection 1 above), in conjunction with the thematic classification of essays (in a later subsection).

3. *The essay as an introduction to figurative uses of language—image, analogy, metaphor, symbol, conceit, and allegory—that pervade all the forms of literature.*

This approach, rather than using the essay to study the distinctive elements of each form, as in the previous approaches, applies the essay to a study of universal elements in literature. Instead of subordinating the essay to the separate forms, this approach subordinates it to a comprehensive and fundamental aspect of form—the figurative quality of literary language. Thus it may be used as the basis for introducing students to the essential qualities of literature prior to their study of the individual literary forms.

To facilitate this approach, we have chosen essays among which there are numerous figurative continuities. Just a brief survey of titles will reveal, for example, that our essays are populated by a host of animals and insects. The world of nature, after all, is a pervasive source of figurative language in literature, for it is a universal source of experience and knowledge shared by all writers and readers. Thus we have emphasized it in our collection of essays. Within that general emphasis we have highlighted particular continuities, as in the three "moth" essays (Woolf's "The Death of the Moth," Thurber's "The Moth and the Star," and Dillard's

"The Death of a Moth"), and the two "chicken" essays (Lawrence's "Cock-sure Women and Hensure Men" and White's "Spring"). Other essays contain a host of animals, such as Mark Twain's "In the Animals' Court," while others play upon the general quality of animalishness, such as Swift's "A Modest Proposal" and Thomas's "The Iks." A few have no counterparts but are present simply because they embody brilliant figurative evocations of nature, such as Thoreau's "The War of the Ants," Orwell's "Shooting an Elephant," and Eiseley's "The Bird and the Machine."

Within any of these sets of essays, you can quickly begin to explore with your students the nature and impact of figurative language—how it is used in literature both to convey experience and to express attitudes, feelings, and ideas about experience. You can also use any of the sets to distinguish between different types of figurative language and the different effects they produce. Perhaps the best way to introduce such an approach would be to have your students read pages 1273–79 and 1289–96 in the critical section, for these contain not only the two "chicken" essays but also a discussion of their different figurative techniques and effects. Lawrence, for example, begins with an image of a typical chicken yard, turns it into an analogy to what he calls the "vast human farmyard," and then extends his analogy into a conceit, so as to make a case against the woman's rights movement of his time. White, by contrast, begins with a detailed image of himself tending a brood of chicks on a cold winter night, and from that image he moves first playfully and then seriously to invoking "the egg" and "the contents of the egg" as symbols of "the necessity for pursuing whatever fire delights you." Once your students have had a chance to examine our commentary on the different types and effects of figurative language in these two essays, you can assign one of the sets in the collection for independent reading, class discussion, or a written assignment. The three "moth" essays, for example, all focus on the theme of death, but explore it through different figurative techniques, and thus provide a set rich in possibilities for analysis.

In connection with this approach, you might also have your students read "Point of View and Language" (pp. 15–19) in the critical section on fiction, as well as "Some Varieties of Metaphorical Language" (pp. 436–43) in the critical section on poetry. These two brief sections will provide your students not only with additional terms and concepts for distinguishing among various types of figurative language, but also with additional illustrations and methods of analyzing figurative language.

THEMATIC

In choosing essays as well as the other texts in our anthology, we have aimed to produce as many thematic continuities as possible. And we have sought to define themes that are of abiding concern, rather than of passing interest, to students and teachers. Thus the six thematic areas under which we have classified essays are: "Death and Dying," "Man and Animal," "Men and Women," "Politics and Society," "War and Peace," "White and Non-White." As these classifications quickly show, we have deliberately striven to define our categories as simply as possible, so as to make them as flexible, as suggestive, and as useful as possible to you, without misleading you about the contents of the works themselves. In line with our commitment to flexibility and accurate representation of themes, we have not tried to force works into a single thematic classification, when they are evidently related to several thematic clusters. Thus you will find that we have classified many of the essays under more than one category. And works that are so classified will immediately be revealed as being thematically rich rather than single-minded.

In our own teaching we have found that *thematic* continuities work very effectively when they are joined with *formal* continuities. Thus if you use the following thematic classification in conjunction with the formal classifications (in subsection 1 above) and the figurative sets (in subsection 3 above), you will be able to prepare a tightly organized formal and thematic sequence for your students. Here, then, is a thematic classification of the essays in our collection.

Death and Dying
FORSTER, "Our Graves at Gallipoli"
ORWELL, "Shooting an Elephant"
WOOLF, "The Death of the Moth"
THURBER, "The Moth and the Star"
DILLARD, "The Death of a Moth"

Man and Animal
WHITE, "Spring"
ORWELL, "Shooting an Elephant"
EISELEY, "The Bird and the Machine"
GREGORY, "If You Had to Kill Your Own Hog"
DILLARD, "The Death of a Moth"

Men and Women
LAWRENCE, "Cocksure Women and Hensure Men"
EPHRON, "The Hurled Ashtray"
DIDION, "On Going Home"

Politics and Society
LAWRENCE, "Cocksure Women and Hensure Men"
EPHRON, "The Hurled Ashtray"
FORSTER, "Our Graves at Gallipoli"
SWIFT, "A Modest Proposal"
TWAIN, "In the Animals' Court"

APPROACHES TO EACH ESSAY IN THE COLLECTION

Here as elsewhere in this manual our comments are meant to be suggestive rather than exhaustive. Thus you will not find in this section an inter-
minable listing of every question that might be asked about each essay.
But you will find some helpful ideas for teaching them—ideas that have
worked for us both in class discussions and in written assignments. And
you will also find some comments that supplement the formal, figurative,
and thematic classifications we have made in the preceding sections. Because we have already provided commentaries and/or questions for the
Lawrence, Ephron, White, and Forster essays in the critical part of our
essay section, we will confine ourselves here to essays in the collection.

JONATHAN SWIFT, "A Modest Proposal" (pp. 1306–13)

The outlandish and outrageous nature of the proposal put forward in the
essay will obviously trouble and perplex many students as it has generations of readers, particularly given the calm, sincere, and apparently rational manner in which it is presented. Thus you will probably find it
necessary to deal with the ironic nature of the essay right off. And you
might find it useful to approach this problem in the context of essayistic
role-playing. Usually, of course, essayists try to put their best foot forward,
projecting an admirable personality that readers are expected to regard as
an aspect of their true self. Sometimes, however, essayists choose to project a disagreeable or despicable personality, one that appears to be stupid
or downright evil. In such cases they are engaged in an act of impersona-
tion, and they expect readers to view the speaker as a character different
from themselves. They also expect readers to regard the speaker's opin-

ions as different from their own. Thus the speaker and the essayist exist not in a direct but in an ironic relation to each other.

Once you have led students to recognize this important distinction, you might invite them to examine the essay with an eye to locating details in it that will enable them to distinguish between Swift and the modest proposer. In looking for such details, they should be attentive to both content and style. They should look for passages or sections which indicate Swift's real view of the issues, as well as his implicit view of the proposer's ideas. They should also consider the extent to which an ironic essay depends upon the author and reader sharing certain values without question or reservation, and should look for explicit or implicit statements of such values in the essay.

Since the essay is called a "proposal," you might also find it useful to examine it as such. A proposal, for example, always involves a proposer, and students might thus be invited to characterize this proposer. How is their impression of the proposer affected by the content of his statements, as well as by the style of his statements? A proposal also involves the formulation and defense of a proposed course of action. Accordingly, students might be invited to locate the proposition and account for what precedes and follows it in the essay. In other words, how is the structure of the essay related to the persuasive strategy of the proposer? What does he do before making his proposal? What does he do after making his proposal? How does the order in which he does things affect one's impression of him and his proposal? Finally, of course, students should be invited to examine and identify the arguments that the proposer offers in support of his proposal, in answer to possible objections that might be raised against his proposal, and in refutation of alternative proposals to his. This detailed examination of the arguments should help students to recognize that Swift's actual views are to be found among both the possible objections and the alternatives.

Once students understand the ironic nature of the essay, they may well admire it so much as to welcome the opportunity to do an imitation. Thus you might invite them to use Swift's technique to write a "modest proposal" of their own on some contemporary situation. Having written such an essay, they might then be invited to discuss how the act of assuming an alien and hostile personality has affected their compositional task.

HENRY DAVID THOREAU, "The War of the Ants" (pp. 1313–16)

Though this piece is excerpted from *Walden,* it has the autonomy of a self-contained essay, and thus can be analyzed in terms of its own distinctive form and the elements of which it is made. We have classified it as a narrative essay because it records in painstaking chronological and physical detail "a war" that Thoreau witnessed "between two races of ants." Yet the most fascinating element of the piece, as our preceding quotation suggests, is its figurative language, for the metaphors of war, as well as of racial and political conflict, are so extensively elaborated in the piece as to constitute a conceit—in fact, an epic conceit. Thus a discussion or written assignment might first be focused on identifying all of the words and phrases that contribute—explicitly and implicitly—to the extended metaphors, and then on analyzing the implications of the extended metaphors. The metaphors in effect constitute a form of commentary on the narrative, but exactly what Thoreau is trying to convey through them remains a nice problem for analysis. Is he trying to make a statement about the horrors of war? Or is he trying to convey the heroic quality of existence in a domain of the natural world—the world of insects—where we would least expect to find it? Or does he intend the metaphors as a source of commentary on racial conflict in the American life of his time?

Once the piece has been examined as a self-contained essay, it can then be discussed within its immediate context, specifically Chapter 12 of *Walden,* which is entitled "Brute Neighbors." In that chapter Thoreau offers detailed descriptions of the activities of several natural creatures—squirrels, partridges, otters, ants, cats, and loons—all living very peaceable lives except the ants. Discussion then might focus on whether an interpretation of the piece is altered by considering the context in which it appears.

MARK TWAIN, "In the Animals' Court" (pp. 1316–18)

This little beast fable in quasi-dramatic form raises a large number of questions for discussion. For example, if we try to translate the figurative terms of the fable into their literal counterparts, we are faced with the immediate question of exactly what kind of law court and legal proceeding Mark Twain actually has in mind. Specifically, is he satirizing divine law, human law, or human interpretation of the Scriptures? In any case, what is his reason for criticizing the law? Is he concerned with the inequity of the laws themselves? They do apparently fail to take into account the unalterably different nature of the beings who are judged according to them. Or is he concerned with the inequity in the system by which the laws are applied? (In the final case of the machine, for example, an exception to the law is granted by the judge.) Or is Mark Twain poking fun at the moral inconsistency of a legal system which ultimately puts the highest value on patriotism, private property, and machines?

These questions can probably best be explored through a careful examination of the form of the essay. How, for example, is one to explain the selection and arrangement of the creatures who appear before the court? Similarly, how is one to explain the relative length with which each of the cases is represented? Finally, how is one to explain the fact that the piece begins like a court report (a narrative summary of the proceedings), but ends like a court transcript (a dramatic record of the dialogue)?

For a different formal approach to a similar problem of values, you might have your students read and compare Gregory's "If You Had to Kill Your Own Hog" (pp. 1341–43). Mark Twain's fable might be compared also to Thurber's "The Moth and the Star" (p. 1321), as well as to the fables and parables in the fiction section (pp. 25–29).

VIRGINIA WOOLF, "The Death of the Moth" (pp. 1318–20)

Here is an essay that runs on for slightly more than two pages, focusing exclusively on the death of a moth—a creature so mundane, so insignificant, that most of us would probably not have paid any attention to its dying had we been witnesses to the event. Yet Virginia Woolf manages to engage our interest in its predicament and to sustain our interest throughout her piece. Indeed, by the end of her narrative she manages to convince us that the death of the moth is fraught with enormous significance, for an understanding both of death and of life. Thus discussion of the essay might well be given over to analysis of the organizational, descriptive, and stylistic techniques by which Woolf develops our interest in the moth and endows its dying with symbolic significance. In connection with this problem, students might be invited to distinguish between the flow of events concerning the death of the moth and the flow of Woolf's thoughts concerning its dying, to see how they are woven together to create the final symbolic effect of the piece.

Woolf's essay might well be studied in conjunction with Doris Lessing's short story, "A Sunrise on the Veld" (pp. 325–32), which narrates a similar kind of experience—that of a boy who comes upon the body of a dying buck—and develops similar insights about life and death. Woolf's essay might also be studied in connection with Auden's poem, "Musée des Beaux Arts" (p. 614), which offers a similar view about the poignantly familiar context of suffering and death, "how it takes place/ While someone else is eating or opening a window or just walking dully along."

JAMES THURBER, "The Moth and the Star" (p. 1321)

This little piece from Thurber's collection, *Fables for Our Time*, might well be studied in connection with the traditional fables of Aesop in the fiction section (pp. 26–27). One question that might be raised about all of the fables is whether they are classified more properly as essays or as stories. Is the moral in each more important than the story, or the story more important than the moral? Or is it impossible to separate one from the other? Would our answers to these questions be the same for the Aesop fables as for Thurber's fable?

Students might be asked to imagine how they would respond to Thurber's fable if he had not provided a moral for it. Would they have seen the story as having the same moral significance? If they had their choice, would they prefer a different moral to be attached to the story? In this connection the class might be invited to supply a list of alternative morals, and discussion might focus on the appropriateness of the alternatives in terms of both their stylistic and their thematic ingenuity. A similar group exercise might be tried on Mark Twain's "In the Animals' Court" (pp. 1316–18), since it too is a fable, but a fable without an explicitly formulated moral.

Finally, students might be asked to consider how their reaction to Thurber's fable is affected by their prior childhood experience of fables such as Aesop's. Is it possible that the humor and the power of Thurber's fable depends upon its witty adaptation of the traditional literary conventions associated with the fable? In this connection, students might be asked whether they think Thurber's moral is to be taken literally (as is the case in traditional fables), or whether it is itself a metaphor which requires interpretation.

GEORGE ORWELL, "Shooting an Elephant" (pp. 1322–28)

This classic work provides a rich set of possibilities for discussing the relationship between story and commentary, as well as between author and fictional self, in a narrative essay. The entire story of Orwell's shooting the elephant runs from the third paragraph of the piece through the penultimate paragraph, yet in the middle of the essay, in the seventh paragraph, just before he is about to shoot the elephant, Orwell reveals the point of his story: "And it was at this moment, as I stood there with my rifle in my hands, that I first grasped the hollowness, the futility of the white man's dominion in the East. . . . I perceived in this moment that when the white man turns tyrant is is his own freedom that he destroys. He becomes a sort of hollow, posing dummy, the conventionalized figure of a sahib." Once Orwell has narratively demonstrated and defined his point, why then does he continue the essay any longer? Why does he subject us—and himself—to retelling all of those gruesome details pertaining to the death throes of the elephant and to his own inability to put the beast out of its miseries?

Another way of considering this same problem is to compare the narrative before the shooting with the narrative that follows it. The narrative before the shooting focuses almost exclusively on Orwell's interior mental processes as he deliberates whether or not to shoot the elephant, whereas the narrative after the shooting focuses almost exclusively on the physical agonies of the elephant. If Orwell's purpose is to explore the impact of imperialism on the white man, why does he laboriously detail its effect upon the elephant? Or is it possible that the white man's powerlessness is most dramatically—and poignantly—revealed in Orwell's fumbling inability even to do a competent job of shooting the elephant?

Orwell's autobiographical essay naturally raises questions about the relationship between author and fictional self, particularly in a case such as this where the author tells an incriminating story about himself. What role, for example, does Orwell play in presenting the essay? and how is that role related to the way he portrays himself at that earlier time when he shot the elephant? Does Orwell the storyteller appear to be a different person from Orwell the elephant shooter? Does he, for example, appear to pass judgment on himself? Does he seem to be telling the story as an act of expiation, as, for example, the Ancient Mariner does in Coleridge's poem? Or does he, instead, seek to engage our sympathy for his predicament? Or does he seem to waver between sympathy and judgment? In considering these questions, particular attention should be paid to the first two paragraphs and the final paragraph of the essay.

LOREN EISELEY, "The Bird and the Machine" (pp. 1329–35)

Though we have classified this as a meditative essay, it might well be considered a persuasive piece, since it makes a very compelling case against the contemporary faith in technology, particularly against the belief that automata and computers might one day match or exceed the capacities of animals and human beings. It might also be classified as a narrative essay, for it tells a very moving story about a memorable experience that Eiseley underwent as a young anthropologist exploring life in the American desert. We prefer to see it as a meditative essay, because Eiseley so clearly projects himself from the very beginning as someone in the act of remembering and reflecting upon experience that he does not even seem to take account of the conventional expectations which readers might have of an essayist to announce his subject and purpose. In his opening sentence, for example, we find him musing upon "their little bones," without any sense of whose "little bones" he has in mind. In the next sentence, he ruminates upon the destiny of "their feathers," from which we infer that he must be thinking about some birds that he witnessed in the past, and finally in the third sentence he makes clear that this is the case. But the entire paragraph is far more taken up with Eiseley thinking about the process of his thoughts than about the birds themselves, about what called the birds to his mind rather than the destiny of the birds. And so the essay progresses throughout its first section, one thought suggesting another, until Eiseley seems to have forgotten the birds altogether and is worrying about the new world of machines and the history of scientific attempts to create machines that might match the capacities of living beings. But his thinking of machines vs. animals does make him return again to the birds, though in thinking about them he also recalls what he learned about "the lesson of time first of all." And this recollection leads him into the first part of his story, which seemingly again leads him away from the birds, though it will inevitably take him back to the birds and the story that climaxes the essay.

As the preceding summary suggests, the process of this essay is very circuitous, as circuitous as is the mind itself in the process of recalling and thinking about past experiences. Thus you might invite students to trace each of the associative moves that Eiseley makes in the process of telling about his thoughts at the breakfast table. Having traced the process of his thoughts, students might then be invited to reflect upon how they are affected by the circuitous, meditative process of the essay. Would they have preferred, for example, to have been told the story of the birds right off, without any of the material that precedes it? Would they have found the story so surprising and moving had Eiseley told it straightforwardly, omitting, for example, the initial musings and possibly even the story of his time up in the canyons with the snake? Would they have found the story so significant without this context and without the process through which the context is established? Ultimately, of course, they should recognize that the very form of the piece not only interprets the story, but provides an instance of the special capacities that machines will never be able to duplicate, namely the processes of thought and feeling distinctive of human beings. In this sense, the form of Eiseley's essay is imitative, reflecting, as does the story of the birds, the things in life that he most values.

For another work that reflects the meditative process of a human being recalling and thinking about past experience, you might invite students to read and compare *Krapp's Last Tape* in the drama collection.

LEWIS THOMAS, "The Iks" (pp. 1336–38)

This concise view of human society and the nature of man embodies an ingenious variation on the typical metaphoric strategy of the argumentative essay. Rather than developing an analogy of his own, Thomas takes an already existing one, refutes its assumptions, and then uses it to develop another analogy for the purposes of arguing a contrary position. The original analogy invoked the Iks—a "small tribe of . . . formerly nomadic hunters"—as "symbols for" what human beings are like in their "inner selves," as well as for how human beings behave when the structure of their society "comes all unhinged." Thomas rejects the analogy because it is based on the "speculative assumption" that man is "fundamentally a bad lot." Instead he chooses to see the Iks as symbolizing "the way groups of one size or another, ranging from committees to nations, behave." That, in short, is what Thomas's essay is about. And your students will be able to catch its drift quite easily.

But they will probably not be so quick to detect the strategies by which Thomas discredits the original analogy and arouses sympathy for his own. Thus discussion might best be focused not only on the competing analogies, but also on the tact and the tactics with which Thomas makes his appeals. In part he discredits the original analogy by arousing scorn for the anthropologist who first proposed it. Thus students might be asked to note each of the points at which Thomas refers to the anthropologist, and consider how each of these references colors our impression of the anthropologist's analogy. He also arouses our distrust of the original analogy by presenting it so as to imply that the anthropologist would consider us readers to be as repulsive as the Iks—"this is what the rest of us are like in our inner selves, and we will all turn into Iks when the structure of our society comes all unhinged." Thus students should be invited to notice the frequency with which Thomas uses the first-person plural pronoun in presenting the anthropologist's analogy, as opposed to the number of times he uses it in presenting his own version of the analogy. Finally, students should be asked to consider the implied personality of Thomas during each of the major sections of his essay—first, when he is refuting the anthropologist, and second, when he is presenting his own view of human nature and society. What kind of personality is implied by the following sentence, for example, which appears at the beginning of Thomas's second section:

I have a theory, then.

And what kind of tone is created by these sentences which appear at the end of his essay?

The Ik, in his despair, is acting out his failure, and perhaps we should pay closer attention. Nations themselves become too frightening to think about, but we might learn some things by watching these people.

In considering the opposing analogies, students might be invited to examine how Thomas uses the same set of details concerning the behavior of the Iks, first to discredit the anthropologist's view of human nature and then to support his own view of human societies. In examining these details, students who are familiar with the fourth book of *Gulliver's Travels* will no doubt detect an arresting similarity between the Iks and the Yahoos, and it might prove interesting to pursue the comparison so as to discover where Swift would stand in this argument between Thomas and the anthropologist. One final question: Why does Thomas use "Ikness" and "Iklike" but never "Ikky" in making his case?

NORMAN MAILER, "A Statement for *Architectural Forum*" (pp. 1338–40)

Mailer's essay is concerned with a distinctive element of contemporary culture—modern architecture—and its impact on the psychic "lives of men and women." Thus it might well be studied in conjunction with Didion's essay on home and family in contemporary culture (pp. 1343–45), particularly because it can also be compared to them in terms of its major elements of form. Mailer's essay, like Didion's, develops a sustained contrast between past and present—between old and new styles of architecture. But Mailer uses his form for argumentative rather than meditative purposes. Thus his essay can be used in conjunction with Didion's to show how similar formal elements can be used to create completely different literary effects. In connection with this kind of analysis, students might also be invited to compare the implied personality—the style and tone—of Mailer with that of Didion. The stark contrast between Mailer's strident voice and Didion's quietly reflective air will give them an immediate clue to the differing purposes and effects of these essayists.

A separate study of Mailer's essay might well be devoted to its figurative language and to the patterns of its prose style. Students might be asked, to begin with, to locate every instance in which Mailer uses the metaphor of totalitarianism, both explicitly and implicitly. Then they might be asked to consider Mailer's reasons for invoking that metaphor. What associations does the word automatically arouse in their minds? Which of these associations does Mailer appeal to in the way he uses the metaphor throughout the essay? In examining Mailer's prose style, students might be invited to identify each of the sentences that develops by accumulating long lists of nouns or adjectives. How frequently does this kind of sentence occur in the essay? In what kind of context does it appear? What kind of tone does it create? What kind of relationship does it establish with a reader? Once these elements of metaphor and prose style have been examined separately, they should be studied jointly in the context of Mailer's overall argumentative purpose. How appropriate and persuasive are these elements in making his case against modern architecture?

DICK GREGORY, "If You Had to Kill Your Own Hog" (pp. 1341–43)

Though this piece is excerpted from the speeches of Dick Gregory, it has the autonomy of a self-contained essay, and thus it can be examined in terms of its own distinctive form. We have classified it as an argumentative essay because it is based on an analogy between animal experience and human experience—an analogy that is introduced at the beginning of the third paragraph:

There is so little basic difference between animals and humans. The process of reproduction is the same for chickens, cattle, and humans. If suddenly the air stopped circulating on the earth, or the sun collided with the earth, animals and humans would die alike.

But one of the most fascinating aspects of the piece is that Gregory uses this analogy to argue two separate points. First, he uses it to argue against killing animals for food:

The day I decide that I must have a piece of steak to nourish my body, I will also give the cow the same right to nourish herself on human beings.

Then he uses it to argue against the conditions of life in the ghetto:

I see no difference between a man killing a chicken and a man killing a human being, by overwork and forcing ghetto conditions upon him, both so that he can eat a little better.

Given these two distinct points, students might well be asked to identify which is the main point, which the subordinate, or whether the two are reciprocally related and part of a larger purpose. In connection with this problem, attention should be called to the narrative framework within which the analogy is introduced and developed. The narrative situation is established in the opening sentences of the piece:

My momma could never understand how white folks could twist the words of the Bible around to justify racial segregation. Yet she could read the Ten Commandments, which clearly say, "Thou shalt not kill," and still justify eating meat.

Gregory again describes his mother's inconsistent appeals to the Bible in the final paragraph, and concludes with these reflections:

When you get involved with distorting the words of the Bible, you don't have to be bitter. The same tongue can be used to bless and curse men.

It is possible, then, that Gregory's essay should be interpreted as being primarily concerned not with the brutality of killing animals for food, nor with the inhumanity of the living conditions inflicted upon blacks by whites, but with the immorality that results from inconsistently interpreting the Bible—or any other moral code, for that matter? If so, then Gregory's essay might be seen as exposing the unethical effects of illogical—or inconsistent—arguments. Thus it seems especially appropriate to consider the logical consistency of Gregory's argument. Once he is granted his basic analogy, does he then develop and apply it consistently?

For another essay which is explicitly concerned with the problem of defining, developing, and applying analogies, you might have your students read and prepare Lewis Thomas's "The Iks" (pp. 1336–38).

JOAN DIDION, "On Going Home" (pp. 1343–45)

Didion's essay is pervaded by a contrast between "home" and "house"—between the rich complications of life in an extended family and the trivial quality of existence in the fragmented world of a large modern city. But the contrast itself is not so compelling as the method by which Didion brings us to feel the truth it contains—no matter whether we grew up in a "home" or a "house." She seems to be narrating an experience—the experience of going "home for my daughter's first birthday." Thus students might be tempted to regard this as a narrative essay. But they should be asked whether the essay actually tells a story about that particular experience, or whether it uses that particular occasion to meditate on the nature of "home" and on the nature of "going home." Didion does begin and end her essay by referring to her daughter's first birthday, but in between she seems to focus less upon that particular event than upon the general drift of events whenever she goes home. And that drift seems inevitably to draw her away from the present life with her husband, seems to draw her back into the past—the irretrievable past—of her family. Thus in discussing the essay students might be invited to examine carefully the sequence of activities that Didion describes in the third, fourth, and fifth paragraphs of her essay, so as to help them see the tension between past and present that she is evoking in her essay.

Once students have seen the powerful—and admittedly painful—hold that the past perennially exerts on Didion, then they will be able to understand why she sets that description of her activities at "home" within the context of the particular visit occasioned by her daughter's first birthday. What, after all, could be a more poignant reminder of an irretrievable past than a young child to whom one would like to pass it on? Thus Didion "would like to give her *home* for her birthday," but she recognizes that "we live differently now and I can promise her nothing like that."

This essay will probably speak more directly to all of your students than any other in the collection. Thus they might well be invited to consider whether Didion's idea of "home"—and of "going home"—corresponds to their own. Indeed, they might well be invited to write their own essays "on going home," essays in which they seek to evoke the particular meaning that "home" has for them.

ELDRIDGE CLEAVER, "The Blood Lust" (pp. 1346–48)

Given the metaphor of boxing that pervades this piece and the explicitly persuasive purpose to which it is put, this is a clear-cut case of an argumentative essay. Still, the process by which Cleaver elaborates the metaphor and the various purposes it serves make this a somewhat more complex essay than it appears at first sight. Initially, the metaphor seems to be intended as a means of defining and expressing the dominantly competitive aspect of American capitalistic society, but as the essay develops it becomes clear that the metaphor is intended to convey something far more convulsive and disturbing in American culture, namely the "blood lust," the violence that Cleaver perceives to be a seminal principle in America. And then finally it is turned into a metaphor for racial and sexual problems afflicting American life. Thus the metaphor turns out to be multifarious in its significance. Given this complexity, you might invite students to trace the development and application of the metaphor throughout the piece, suggesting that they also attempt to account for the process by which Cleaver moves from one aspect of its significance to the next. You might also ask them to identify which of its significances they believe to be most important for Cleaver.

Given its concern with the nature and causes of racial conflict, Cleaver's essay might well be compared to Gregory's essay, as well as to Langston Hughes's play in the drama collection, *Mother and Child*. For another perspective, you might have students read it in connection with *The Threepenny Opera*, since both works are fierce attacks on the savage effects of capitalistic society.

ANNIE DILLARD, "The Death of a Moth" (pp. 1348–51)

Though this is one of the shorter essays in the collection, it is also one of the most complex. But if it is approached systematically, your students will probably also find it to be one of the most rewarding. We suggest that it be examined section by section, and these can easily be noted by the spatial breaks that appears on pages 1349 and 1350. Thus you might begin by asking your students to explain what Dillard's primary topic is in each section. Their initial response to that question will most likely be a literal explanation of what Dillard reports in each section. They will probably focus on her meticulous description of the insect carcasses in the first section; on her equally detailed narration of the moth burning in the candle flame in the second section; and on her unusually frank report of her personal feelings about living alone in the third section. These literal descriptions of each section should be encouraged, because they will quickly bring to the surface a central problem in understanding the essay. Specifically, what is the connection of that final section to the other two? Why does Dillard suddenly shift from describing the death of insects to reporting personal feelings about her solitary life? What does the quality of her life have to do with the death of a moth? Logically, of course, they have nothing to do with one another, but experientially and figuratively they are intimately related.

One way of helping students to discover the relationship might be to call their attention to the fact that Dillard begins her essay by asserting "I live alone"—that the essay thus begins and ends by focusing on the quality of her life. Then they might be asked to notice that the second section also opens with statements that describe her life, in particular how she was inspired to be a writer by Rimbaud, whom she later speaks of as having "burnt out his brain in a thousand poems." Once these details are called to their attention, then they will probably be able to recognize that she intends her painstaking description of the moth burning in the candle flame—a description which focuses particularly on the "moth's head" burning for two hours—to be seen as a metaphor for her own life and her own aspirations. Thus it is that she can claim to be an expert on moths, to "know what moths look like, in any state," for she has not only witnessed them closely under many circumstances, but she has also "had some experience with the figure Moth reduced to a nub." And that concentrated impression of herself, embodied in "the figure Moth," is exactly what she gives us in the essay.

Film

MICHAEL SILVERMAN

THE ELEMENTS OF FILM

Film can usefully be linked with drama and prose fiction, since it combines theatricality and narrativity as essential "problematic" components. Many students, in fact, will have had their first exposure to narrative through visual media. The use of film in a basic Humanities course may then have the initial appeal to the student of something familiar—but when this object is put under close scrutiny by an instructor the appeal to familiarity may give way, to be replaced by a desire for analysis. A simple narrative phenomenon, such as the manner in which one event succeeds the preceding one, may not initially be identified as a "problem" at all. If it *is* to be seen as a problem—e.g., how does the work move from point *A* to point *B*? how does it move the reader's affective response?—the superficial acceptance (and the mere acceptance of surfaces) has to be blasted away. Film can aid in posing narrative and theatricality as a problem, because although it may seem like relaxation and a diversion away from the preoccupations of literature, it in fact locates the student precisely within a series of problems just when he had thought he was going to take a holiday. Film is in this sense a sneakily effective weapon.

In the present book, film is approached both as an object of study in itself (in order that it may be seen as something not merely ancillary to the more traditional literary forms), and as an extension of the study of literature. To the extent that film shares central preoccupations with other forms, it can be seen as an element of expression which has its own mode of existence but which can be brought into play with and against other elements.

In building bridges between drama, fiction, and film, one might consider the following areas of enquiry:

narrativity in film and fiction (point-of-view, reflexivity, etc.)

character delineation in drama, fiction, and film

absence/presence of an audience in drama and film

position of the spectator in drama and film, of the reader in fiction (and poetry)

One might utilize the following as specific points of contact across the anthology sections as a whole:

biography as metafiction (*Citizen Kane* and "Lost in the Funhouse"

the depiction of an object and the nature of illusion (Welles's sled, Lawrence's rocking horse)

the sense of loss and false renewal (repetition and desire in the "snow scene" of *Citizen Kane* and Rich's "Amnesia") visual depiction (with reference both to film as representation and to the gallery images in Marvell's "The Gallery" or Auden's "Musée des Beaux Arts")

the foregrounding of character (the tug toward naturalism in essentially nonnaturalistic works: *Citizen Kane* and *The Stronger*)

morality tales ancient and modern (*Everyman, Cat on a Hot Tin Roof, Citizen Kane*)

the spectator's passivity in the face of the event (*Oedipus Rex, Citizen Kane*)

AVAILABILITY

If you decide to spend time incorporating *Citizen Kane* with your course, you should reserve a print of the film at least 2–3 months in advance of the date you wish to show it. At least three major distributors rent prints of the film (Films, Incorporated; MacMillan Audio Brandon; Janus Films; see addresses at end of this discussion) and each of them has regional offices. Cost and quality of prints will vary. If you wish your students to see the film more than once, or if you wish particular segments of the film to be screened several times, you should talk things over with the distributor. Stress that the film will be used for classroom purposes only, with no admission charged; in doing so you will be eligible for any special educational rate. You will find that the degree of cooperation will vary from firm to firm; at times it is worth paying a few dollars extra in order to ensure good print quality and a flexible attitude toward screenings.

USE

In its current state, film is more unwieldy as a text than any book. Students tend to miss the direct access to the materials, the ability to scan back and forth. It is essential that the instructor maintain as much control as possible over the film as a physical object and over the conditions of its showing. If you simply turn the film over to an Audiovisual technician, and let a screening be arranged under "normal" conditions, you will begin to experience a feeling of helplessness. You must try to secure a projector and screen, find a competent operator, and reserve for yourself the ability to stop or start the screening at any moment. Avoid projectors with automatic loading capacity or those equipped with stop-action (or "freeze frame") capabilities. No matter how economical and attractive they might seem as pedagogical tools, they invariably damage film. An old-fashioned, hand-loaded projector that permits the film to pass lightly through its mechanism is the best sort of machine.

SCREENINGS AND LECTURES

Most instructors teaching film on a regular basis prefer to show a film once to an audience without any preliminary remarks. The student then has the opportunity to absorb the design of the film as a whole and to make initial discoveries that can be confirmed or modified by a second screening, either of the whole film once again or of an individual sequence. There are any number of satisfactory formulas that will enable you to avoid lecturing about a film no one has recently seen (equivalent to lecturing about a novel no one in the class has read). A screening on the evening before a lecture permits time for reflection, and chances are good that on the next day the images will still be fresh in the mind; the lecture itself may be punctuated by specific passages shown as illustration; finally, an additional screening will help students to take close cognizance of material singled out for assignments.

It is often difficult to find the precise passages that are meant for specific illustration: most films are shipped on 1,600-foot reels, and finding the precise 15 or 20 feet of a particular series of shots in the middle of a lecture is certainly frustrating and to all practical intent impossible. You might wish to resort to inserting slips of paper into the take-up reel just at the beginning of an important sequence. Thses slips should be marked with an identifying phrase; at the end of the initial screening, do not re-wind the film, since working "tails out" will enable you to utilize the fast re-wind mechanism of the projector to locate a passage. Very few projectors come equipped with a "fast forward" mechanism.

With a film like *Citizen Kane,* which breaks at precise moments so as to structure itself around various narratives, you may wish to concentrate on a single narrative block for close scrutiny. The blocks overlap, of course, but concentration of this sort will reduce the student frustration at trying to get the story "straight." It can be explained finally that when all individual narratives are fused into the film as a whole, there are still gaps and fissures remaining in the text of Kane's life. But the operations of an individual narrative block may come to stand metonymically for the operation of narrative in the full text.

CONCENTRATING ON ONE NARRATIVE: JED LELAND'S STORY

When Thompson the investigative reporter seeks out Kane's oldest friend, Jed Leland, he has just finished interviewing Bernstein and has heard briefly of the marriage between Kane and Emily Monroe Norton. This marriage provides the link between Bernstein's and Leland's reminiscences. After some preliminary banter about cigars and doctors, Leland indicates prior acquaintance with Emily ("Like all the girls I knew in dancing school"), and we are given a series of four exchanges between Kane and his wife to "illustrate" the marriage. These famous breakfast-table remarks compress about eight years of real time into approximately three minutes of film time.

At first, Leland's figure is held on the screen as a visible reminder that these scenes (though private, and impossible for Leland to have seen literally) stand as "representations" of narration. Much of what we actually see in the film is impossible to ascribe to the eye of any single character, though in *Citizen Kane* there is, precisely, an attempt to make such an ascription. In fact, the entire project of the newspaperman's investigation might be seen as an attempt to find a reliable narrator. We finally understand, though, that if we examine narrative segments as autonomous entities (Leland's story, or Bernstein's) we are getting interesting stories, but not necessarily reliable ones.

Further, if we examine the text of the film at the level of the individual shot within any narrative segment, we can say that it is extremely difficult to ascribe with absolute clarity that shot's point of view. When the camara glides through the window at Xanadu just in time to see the glass globe slip from the hand of the dying Kane, or when it travels upward behind the scenes of Susan Alexander's operatic debut to reveal two stagehands registering distaste, specifically whose viewpoint is being registered by the camera? Either we are being given "privileged" moments by the camera, or we are (to recall many instances that take place within a literally "narrated" framework) in effect at the mercy of the narrator, subject to his or her whims, proclivities, exaggerations.

A concrete list of the events related by Leland to Thompson might help us with the difficulties involved here:

1. Four breakfast conversations between Kane and Emily. (*27 shots, ranging in time from 1901 to 1909*)

This is followed by another direct intervention by Thompson, who does not reappear directly on the screen until Leland tells of Kane's finishing the review of Susan's operatic debut. Thus, everything that follows appears as "straight" narration, though we know that the figure of Leland stands directly (though invisibly) between the audience and the events.

2. Kane and Susan meet on the street outside her apartment. She is suffering from a toothache, and he has just been soaked by a passing carriage. (*1 shot, 1915*)

3. Kane and Susan inside her apartment. He amuses her with shadow-play on the walls, then reveals that he was on his way "to the Western Manhattan Warehouse, in search of my youth." That he and Susan both had mothers who were ambitious for them seems deeply significant to Kane. (*20 shots*)

4. Kane persuades Susan to play the piano in the parlor and sing. She struggles as Kane sits sunken in a wing chair, the epitome of bourgeois domestic contentment. Smoke wreathes about his head, he slowly and complacently applauds her efforts. (*2 shots*)

Events 2, 3, and 4 follow in direct succession. But the single applause of Kane for Susan begins to merge into the cheers of thousands at the political rally in Kane's electoral campaign. The following "scenes" are connected by sound, through a series of "lightning mixes."

5. Leland addresses a few people gathered in the corner of neighborhood lot. Only one person shouts for Kane, though there is sporadic applause. (*1916, beginning of campaign; 1 shot*)

6. Kane finishes a sentence by Leland, though this shot succeeds the former by an

indeterminate number of weeks. He addresses a huge rally, in the presence of his wife and son. We do not know that the wife knows of Kane's affair with Susan. We do not at this point even have ocular proof that an affair between Kane and Susan exists. Toward the end of this sequence, the camera is located in a high box overlooking the rally (here R-K-O and Welles use a painted backdrop), and we see a man who looks down and quickly exits. He will be revealed in a few minutes as Kane's opponent, Boss Jim Gettys. (*17 shots; 1916*)

7. A triumphant Kane looks for his wife and child. He is informed by Emily that she is going to 185 West 74th Street. We still do not know that the affair has been discovered; our sympathies are with Kane, but we can detect a shift in the balance of power. Kane goes with his wife. (*15 shots*)

8. When Kane is greeted by name by the maid at the door, the discovery is fully unveiled (though of course Kane knew the moment Emily read the address from a slip of paper). Emily, Gettys, Kane, and Susan confront each other. Kane decides to stay in the election. (*16 shots*)

Events 6, 7, and 8 occur on the same evening, with relatively short intervals of time between them. The amount of time elapsing between 8, 9, and 10 is much more indeterminate—possibly one or two days separating 8 and 9, a week or so separating 9 and 10. However, the fact that Leland is shown entering a saloon at the end of 9 and is still drunk during the crucial conversation with Kane at 11 leaves us with two choices: either 9, 10, and 11 follow each other in rapid succession, or Leland has been on a rather extended drunken binge. If the latter is seen as a possibility, Leland's drunkenness on the night of Susan's debut is de-sentimentalized, as it were. That is, he's not drunk because he doesn't want to write a bad review about an old friend's wife, or because he's afraid of losing his job—he is drunk simply out of what by now is confirmed habit.

9. The *Chronicle*, the rival paper, which Kane had depleted of its best staff, gets its revenge by breaking the story of the "love nest." Leland sees the headline and enters a saloon. (*2 shots*)

10. Bernstein and the *Examiner* staff concede defeat by claiming fraud. (*1 shot*)

11. Leland confronts Kane with the reasons for his defeat, as he sees them, in the deserted election headquarters. Kane wants love, but only "on your own terms . . . according to your rules." Leland asks to be transferred to the Chicago edition of the paper; Kane assents, and drinks to "love on my terms." (*3 shots; night turns to daybreak during the conversation*)

12. Kane marries Susan, with reporters gathering around. Kane already addresses one as "young man," as if he himself has aged considerably in a few weeks. He announces plans for Susan's operatic career. (*1 shot; possibly late 1916 or early 1917*)

13. Susan's debut, which will be shown in greater detail in Susan's own narrative, which follows immediately. Here confusion reigns, and quick succession punctuated almost at once by the stagehands' reactions. (*3 shots; 1919*)

Events 12 and 13 compress Susan's training and Kane's retirement from public affairs into four shots. Indeed, the first shot of thirteen is merely a sign reading "Kane Builds Opera House," a refutation of Kane's parting shot to a reporter who had asked him if in fact he had any plans to build an opera house: "That won't be necessary."

14. The office of the Chicago *Enquirer*, with Bernstein imported specially from New York to supervise the operatic event. Kane enters, is told that every "notice" but the dramatic is ready. Kane and Bernstein discover Leland sprawled in a drunken sleep on top of his typewriter, the notice half-finished. (*14 shots*)

15. Kane completes Leland's notice, denigrating Susan's talent. The wide angles and deep focus recall the conversation of 11. Kane fires Leland, with an emphatic movement of the typewriter carriage. (*4 shots*)

At this point we return to "present time," with Thompson and Leland sitting on the roof of the hospital. Leland reveals that Kane had written him, but that he had refused to answer. He is led away by two nurses.

In analyzing this or any other narrative, you might try to suggest the differences between literary and cinematic point of view, even when the idea of narrative plays such a marked and determining role in a film. It would be important, too, that the students understand how the slightest visual detail can impinge upon meaning, can be taken up as a narrative detail in itself. Everything treated under specific codes of the cinema, its native elements, moves in a classic Hollywood text to organize a series of images into some narrative arrangement. The interest of *Citizen Kane* lies in part, of course, in its A, looking like a different sort of film but actually conforming in many ways to a standard narrative model, and, contrarily B, seeming to be all about storytelling and narrative, while not giving us the final figure in the carpet.

ADDRESSES OF FILM DISTRIBUTORS

Films, Incorporated
1144 Wilmette Avenue
Wilmette, IL 60091

Janus Films
745 Fifth Avenue
New York, NY 10022

MacMillan Audio Brandon
37 MacQuesten Parkway South
Mount Vernon, NY 10550